AMERICAN REFUGE

AMERICAN REFUGE

True Stories of the Refugee Experience

Diya Abdo

Steerforth Press
Truth to Power Books

LEBANON, NEW HAMPSHIRE

For information about permission to reproduce
selections from this book, write to:
Steerforth Press L.L.C., 31 Hanover Street, Suite 1,
Lebanon, New Hampshire 03766

In 2020, Steerforth Press launched Truth to Power Books: investigative
journalism, iconoclastic histories, and personal accounts that are nuanced,
thoughtful, and reliable — qualities at a premium in the Internet age — and
that inform through storytelling, not argument.

Cataloging-in-Publication Data is available from the Library of Congress

ISBN 978-158642-342-1 (Paperback)

Manufactured in the United States of America

1 3 5 7 9 10 8 6 4 2

To my daughters, Aidana and Seira,

And for my grandmother Sabha, and all the welcomers.

CONTENTS

AUTHOR'S NOTE

Refugees are forced to seek safety elsewhere because home, forever soul-filled and memory-rich, is no longer safe. For refugees, exile is the solution to the problem of death.

And the problem of death is universal, indiscriminate. It can happen to anybody at any time. The relative recency of the term *refugee* in national and international law and the associated conflicts and war zones that have produced refugees have racialized it, interminably intertwined it with certain bodies from certain parts of the world — especially the Global South and the conflict zones in the Middle East and Africa.[1] But in truth, anybody can become a refugee.

The stories you will read in this book were all shared within the context of formal interviews I conducted especially for the purpose of their publication. The interviewees were very clear about what they were excited to share, wanted the world to know, and what they wanted to keep sacred and secret, to me and to themselves. I was very careful to follow their wishes.

1

RADICAL HOSPITALITY

When human beings find themselves compelled to move, who are we to tell them they must stop?

Human beings have always moved — and they have done so largely to survive. The story of human migration is twin to the story of humanity.[1] In search of food, water, pliable and arable land, safety and security, job opportunities, love and companionship, freedom — humans have gathered their disparate selves (within them and without them, their torn souls and their families) and left for destinations both known and unknown.

I come from a people for whom movement is perpetual. As Bedouins, movement was a staple of our past existence, and as Palestinians, it is a staple of our present. In the former, much like the latter, this movement was not by choice. The land around my people dried out, their cattle diminished and disappeared, the sky burned hot. So they tightened for travel[2] — a serious business meant only for serious worship — and they struck out in search of the wet and the cool.

They found it on one of the Mounts of Jerusalem, of which there are four. Theirs is called Jabal Al-Mukaber: the Mountain of the Caller of Allah's Greatness.[3] Now our whole tribe lives there — the Sawahreh — the "travelers," the "tourists." Many of them were made travelers and tourists again when our land burned hot, this time under Israeli occupation. My grandmother tightened for travel, reliving an age-old performance of her people, and gathered herself and her two children — walked with them across the River Jordan to the urban refugee camps of Jordan's Al-Zarqa'a — the Blue City.

Arid, dusty, and impoverished, Al-Zarqaʿa is named after what the travelers hoped to find again — the wetter, the cooler, the greener. They named neighboring hills the Green Mountain and the White Mountain (Al-Jabal Al-Akhdar and Al-Jabal Al-Abyad) — but in truth, they were neither green nor white.

The human desire to name places after that which travelers have left behind is all around us; it inscribes the story of human movement into the very cities and states we find ourselves in right now, generations out from our moving predecessors.[4] And for this country — the United States of America — such naming often erases what came before. The new Yorks and Londons and Jerseys and Englands and Havens tell a story of human migration respected and normalized — the story of the *good* refugees, the *good* immigrants:[5] the white, the European, the Christian. My family comes from a place where a similar renaming is underway. The communities of Katamun, Quds, and Deir Yassin are now known officially by their Hebrew names: Gonen, Urshalim, and Kfar Shaul.[6] That too is a migration respected, normalized, of a people returned to their rightful place.[7] To rename is real, as real as taking ownership of a land from which one has expelled others, as real as forcing the already-there human bodies into their own displacement, their own migration.

Those who now become the *bad* refugees, the *bad* immigrants.

Migration is a human right. When human beings find themselves compelled to move, who are we to tell them they must stop? But when human migration turns into imperialism, colonialism, occupation, genocide, then it is no longer just migration. It is cannibalism: the consumption of the qualities and possessions of the already-there human bodies, what is left of them now regurgitated in another form —the *bad* refugees, the *bad* immigrants.

I was born in Jordan in 1976, the child of Palestinian refugees who were displaced in 1967. My grandmother and mother initially lived in, and then managed to escape, the drudgeries of the refugee camps. Both my paternal and maternal grandparents lived the rest of their lives outside Palestine. Their children gave birth to children who gave birth to children. Many of these children stayed in Jordan, and many others — their identities, their sense of belonging, fractured by the inherited loss of the initial great displacement — tightened for travel and scattered all over the globe.

My cousins currently live in Canada, in South America, in Europe, and in various countries in the Arab world. Like many of my cousins — the children of the displaced — my siblings and I similarly emigrated. My sister lives in Saudi Arabia. My brothers and I live in the United States.

In Arabic, we call an emigrant *muhajir*, the root of which means "to abandon," or *mughtarib*, the root of which means both "strange" and "west" — the estranging direction into which many moving Arab bodies disappear.

Many Palestinians, children of the displaced, have "wested."[8] Their children, like mine and my siblings', are born in these new countries — thrice removed from Palestine. The initial great displacement reverberates through generations.

In 1996, I came to the US as a graduate student on an international visa. I returned to Jordan when life in the US after September 11 became too complicated, too hard, for Arabs and Muslims. The terrorist attacks of September 11 ended so many lives, and they fundamentally changed the trajectory of so many others. As a graduate student, I had initially specialized in twentieth-century American literature. When the attacks happened, I found myself being called upon by many in the community (especially the university where I studied and taught and other communities connected to the university) to explain Arab and Muslim culture, especially Arab and Muslim women's lives and experiences. My interests shifted from American literature to Arab and Islamic feminisms and Arab women writers, and I returned to Jordan to live and teach. It was this new specialization, and one particular publication, that got me in trouble at the Jordanian university where I was teaching at the time. Although I won the battle against the university, this painful violation of my freedom of speech made it too complicated, too hard for me to stay in Jordan.[9] I returned to the US for a teaching position in the South.

In 2015, I was a tenured professor of English at Guilford College in Greensboro, North Carolina. The Syrian refugee crisis was at its zenith, and like the rest of the world, I was shattered by the picture of Alan Kurdi — the three-year-old Syrian boy who drowned, along with his mother and younger brother, when their boat from Turkey to Greece capsized.[10] At the time, Alan was close to the age of my youngest daughter, and many parents I knew saw the bodies of our own children in his waterlogged body.

The rest of the world reacted powerfully to Alan's image.[11] His small body, seriously dressed for a dark and serious passage, mobilized (albeit briefly and insufficiently) politicians and citizens around the world in a way no other image representing the terror and danger of the journey refugees have to make had done before. Hungary, which had been holding back Syrian refugees trying to make their way north, allowed them to cross through, and Austria and Germany accepted those streaming multitudes with open arms.[12]

And Pope Francis called on every parish in Europe to host one refugee family.[13]

In my midsized city of Greensboro, North Carolina, I wondered about the role of academic institutions in such a global crisis. How were we supposed to respond? What were we supposed to do with our shattered hearts? With the endless convoy of humanity trying to make its way from misery to the unknown? What is our responsibility as teachers, students, and administrators of higher learning? What is our complicity as institutions built on the lands of the dispossessed and displaced?

And more specifically, I asked: How could I leverage my position and my institution to do something *material*, something *real*? I had gotten tired of our academic "go-to" after every catastrophe — the panels, the teach-ins, the petition-signing, the lecturing, the public talking, the statement-making. Yes, these actions were necessary and educational, but their effect seemed distant *to* me and *from* me in moments that necessitated urgency. Once completed, these actions were removed from my hands, reverberating instead through generations of students — or so we hoped.

That fall of 2015, I was especially struck by the immediate and material action of the activists who drove all the way down from Austria to Hungary in not-long-enough convoys to bring back up the thousands-too-long convoy of Syrian refugees trying to make their way from Hungary to Germany.

Oh, how I wished I were in Austria with a car.

But then I realized I was somewhere better — a refugee resettlement hub.[14]

With something even better — a college campus.

As I reflected on Pope Francis's invocation to radical hospitality,[15] I remembered (and how could I have forgotten?) that the Arabic word for "campus" is *haram*. It means "sanctuary." And a sudden simple, basic realization came to me: The place where I was, the campus of Guilford College, and indeed every other college and university campus, is exactly like a parish. A campus isn't just the locus of thinking, studying, teaching, and lecturing — a disembodied "life of the mind" as the platitude goes and as one of my colleagues frequently, lovingly reminded me.

A campus is just like a small city — a *place* as much as it is a *mind*. And it is a place with everything necessary to respond to the pope's inspired call on smaller communities to host a refugee family. Residential campuses have housing, cafeterias, clinics, and plenty of human resources, expertise, and connections to provide financial, social, and community support to newcomers trying to make their way from misery to the unknown.

And I knew enough about the misery *of* the unknown. As an adult immigrant to the US and a child of Palestinian refugees who was born and raised in Jordan (the "alternate homeland" as many Palestinians facetiously called it), the desire to tame the miserable unknown into an image of the known, of Palestine, was never far from what I taught, what I named my children, what I cooked at home, what protests I attended. My grandmother had raised me. Her daily nighttime stories — as I lay in the softness of her raised elbow on our shared bed — about the rich intricacies of life in Palestine, the pain of departure and separation from her family members in 1967, and the exclusion and violence Palestinians experienced during the early years of their displacement in Jordan — informed the ways in which I understood the experiences of refugees and the ways in which I did what I did next.

That fall of 2015, I walked into Guilford's president's office and asked for a Guilford College house to host refugees.

Guilford's president very simply said yes, and Every Campus A Refuge was born. I partnered with community organizations, including our local refugee resettlement agencies, designing an initiative to host refugees on our campus grounds and support them in their resettlement. We used all the resources at our community's disposal to create a home, a sense of belonging, a place of radical hospitality. Although the refugee resettlement program is federal, resettlement itself takes place locally, making the most important factor the community into which refugees are received and, hopefully, welcomed. Every Campus A Refuge makes college and university campuses into such welcoming communities.*

Since January 2016 and as of this writing, we have hosted eighty-two refugees on Guilford College's campus —thirty-four of them children — from Afghanistan, Syria, Sudan, Iraq, Uganda, Rwanda, the DRC, Colombia, and Venezuela. Other campuses have joined and are joining the effort, responding to this call for radical hospitality on college and university campuses.

In this book, you will read true stories of refugee experiences. These experiences belong to refugees hosted by Every Campus A Refuge at Guilford College and those who participated as students and volunteers in this hosting effort. The experiences are as varied and diverse as the humans to whom these stories belong. I have come to know all of these individuals personally, and over the years I have formed deep relationships with them, ones animated by trust, love, and friendship. I have come to know their stories of displacement, of waiting in limbo, of resettlement, as I know my own family's.

These stories begin in their home countries, the places and people they never wanted to leave, and travel through the conflicts that caused them to gather their disparate selves and cross borders, first to countries next door and then to countries unknown, much farther away, like dust in the wind, droplets of water, scattered far from home.

These are the stories of unstoppable human beings on the move.

* Research conducted shows a powerful outcome: Refugees hosted by the program at Guilford College reported a greater sense of financial stability and sense of belonging. (Diya Abdo and Krista Craven, "Every Campus A Refuge: A Small College's Engagement with Refugee Resettlement," *Migration and Society: Advances in Research* 1 [2018]: 135–48) Student volunteers reported increased knowledge and understanding of refugee and immigrant issues. (Meriam Mckey et al., "Every Campus A Refuge Volunteer Study," JPS 448 Community and Justice Studies Capstone Seminar, Spring 2020, Guilford College).

2

THE BODY LEAVES ITS SOUL BEHIND

In a land where I do not see you, I am a stranger
My soul stays with you when my body travels
Even among the noise of the throngs, my yearning isolates me
As if I were completely alone in a land with no people
— MOHAMMED AL MUQRIN[1]

Human bodies on the move don't always take their souls with them. Sometimes, they leave their souls behind. Lay them down before they gather their disparate selves and strike out — on planes or cars or inflatable boats or foot to cross borders they must cross to keep themselves and their children safe. If they are lucky, their souls might come to find them — reuniting with them across vast distances. But it is an exhausted union: The body has left the soul for a long time, and their union is a shadow of its former joy.

Often, refugees spend the rest of their lives yearning for that which they have had to leave behind — love, family members, a land bountiful and once theirs, homes that brought them together before fracturing them into the corners of the earth.

When refugees leave, it is rarely, if ever, happy. And it is never something they choose to do.

Their bodies, finding no other way to survive, split themselves from their souls, wave them goodbye on the fragile hope that soon they will meet again.

When I left my grandmother Sabha to come to the United States for the second time in 2008,[2] she told me again, "You have taken my soul with you."

Like all Palestinian refugees, she had practiced soul-leaving many times and was too exhausted by the constant fracture, the never-ending splintering, the recurring emptying out of her flesh from its family members' love and presence. The Israeli occupation of 1948 and its expansion into additional territories in Palestine in 1967 altered her life and her family's history in ways that were irrevocable and generational. It separated her from parents and siblings and displaced her into unwelcoming and hostile lands. This splitting from the soul — from Palestine — is an absence felt by the generations of Palestinians born to displaced and refugee Palestinian parents. Their children and grandchildren, similarly untethered, gathered their unsouled selves and immigrated to the various corners of the earth — Saudi Arabia, the US, Kuwait, Canada, England, Colombia, Peru — wherever planes and ships could take them.

In 2008, the day I got on the plane in Jordan to begin my career at Guilford College in Greensboro, North Carolina, Sabha fell ill. Though an expert at splitting from her soul, this last break was perhaps too much. She was taken to the hospital and never left it; she died two months later, on my birthday, a day after I told her I was pregnant with my first child — a daughter I named after her: Aidana Sabha.

A little fire named after the fiery light of the sun, the morning.*

A pale imitation of re-souling. A fabricated reunion of souls.

My grandmother was displaced from her hometown in the suburbs of Jerusalem in 1967; this displacement is referred to by Arabs generally, and Palestinians specifically, as Al-Naksa, the setback.

Nearly twenty years earlier, in 1948, almost 750,000 people — nearly half of the Palestinian population of the time — were

---

* The name Aidana means "little fire" in Irish, and Sabha comes from the Arabic word "morning" — *sabah*.

made refugees by the Israeli occupation of Palestine. More than
four hundred villages were destroyed or ethnically cleansed,[3] their
populations massacred (as in Deir Yassin and Ayn Zaytun) or
internally displaced elsewhere in Palestine or across its borders in
Jordan, Syria, Lebanon, and Egypt.

This is referred to as Al-Nakba, the catastrophe. A catastrophe
followed by a setback where hundreds of thousands were displaced,
and new refugees created.

In 1967, my grandmother was a young woman in her early thir-
ties and had already seen her fair share of hardship. My extended
family, the Sawahreh, were as diverse as they were numerous,
with varying economic and educational statuses. The Attiyehs, my
grandmother's branch — or "thigh" as they say in Arabic — were
simple folk. She and many of her siblings were illiterate. Their
lives were humble, tied to the land and its bounty, true salt-of-the-
earth peasants. In the same tribe, there were other branches, other
thighs, whose ambitions changed their ways of life. My grandmother married my grandfather — from the Abdos — at a very
young age, too young to say here out loud. He was ambitious and
pursued a prestigious educational path. Initially, she accompanied
him when he became a teacher in the villages of Palestine. But
when he wanted something more for his life, something farther,
he left her to pursue graduate degrees and teaching opportunities,
first in the Arab world and then in the West. By the time she passed
away in 2008, at the age (possibly) of seventy-five, my siblings and
I had taught her how to write her name and how to record people's
phone numbers in a little tattered book she carried around in the
breast pocket of her *thobe*, the traditional Palestinian embroidered
dress she always wore. My grandfather, by then, had become a full
professor of linguistics and phonetics, with publications and acco-
lades too numerous to count, and many wives since Sabha.

My grandmother refused to remarry after her husband left her.
She had with him only two children, a boy and a girl, too few for

the women of the time like her sisters and sisters-in-law, who each had nearly ten children.

Her daughter, my mother, was the age of my oldest daughter right now — twelve years old — when they gathered their small family and crossed the border to Jordan, leaving their souls behind.

Afaf, from Palestine

Afaf, my mother, Sabha's daughter, was born in Jerusalem in 1954. When she returned to visit Palestine in 2019 on her American passport — the only way Israel would allow her to enter the country — she stayed for forty days. This length of stay wasn't intentional on her part, but she always begins her reminiscences with "Those forty days I spent in Palestine." It is an auspicious number for Muslims: Prophet Muhammad spent forty days in spiritual meditation in the cave after the first revelation,[4] and Muslims mourn their dead for forty days — at which point the soul, having separated from the body at the moment of death, is presumed to return for its final visit.

Her return to Palestine for those forty days is no less sacred, no less reviving. Indeed, she describes it as an *isra'*, the Prophet's journey by night on a winged horse to Al-Aqsa Mosque in Jerusalem to lead prayer. "Like a specter," she tells me, "I was allowed by divine intervention to travel by night to Jerusalem." On her pilgrimage, she visited all the sites holy to her; she moved between the neighborhood houses, knocking on their doors, letting them know that she had returned.

"Open the door for me," her specter entreated. "Please. I am Afaf. I have come back."

She knocked on the door of her dead aunt Aisha, who sold milk from the few cows she owned.

As a child, Afaf would walk there in the morning to buy some milk for her mother and brother; and on the way back, she would drink it all because it was so delicious, so warm. In her domed room — an ancient ruin — Aisha sold whatever else she could make of her cows' milk, especially cheese pastries, covered with delicate gauze to keep them warm and clean. On some mornings, Aisha would call out, her voice ringing clearly across the houses that separated her from her sister-in-law: "*Haiy, ya* Sabha. How are you? Come breakfast with me."

She knocked on the door of her dead aunt Fatmeh, who, like all the other women, never made meals just enough for the family to eat. The family was the entire neighborhood because they were all related, all part of the same tribe. One never knew when a cousin or cousins would decide to visit for lunch. And so the door was kept unlocked and the pots of rice bigger than a single family could ever eat.

She knocked on the door of her dead aunt Hamdeh, whose house was built next to a cave. Afaf and her cousin Sara were terrified to go in there, making up songs about their fear and the cave's haunting horrors. But Hamdeh used that cave as she would any other room in her house — she cooked in it, slept in it, received guests in it. When the girls slept in the room next door, they delighted in their fears, and their aunts, obliging, would cover them with quilts and feed them small Egyptian seeds as they told them stories about the Ghoul who lived nearby and the mischievous Hdeidoon who once tricked her by carving out a watermelon and hiding inside of it, sticking out only one of his ears and his penis. He rolled down the hill like a fruit possessed, scaring the Ghoul. The Ghouls were always women. People feared them because they had long hair that ran down their faces and only one eye. But the Ghouls, like the rest of the people in the neighborhood, wanted to live in peace; whatever they did to scare others was done to protect their children.

She knocked on the door of her dead aunt Amneh, who would gather her sisters on the soft grass that grew on the mountainside. On this *jaladeh*, the women would embroider and sing together as they marked their black crepe with the codes of the Jerusalem *thobe* in traditional golden threads — the flowers, the crescents, the trees. When their tongues craved something sweet, there on the mossy blanket, they had no manufactured candy to rely on. All they had in their neighborhood was a small store owned by one of the relatives; he sold date paste that came in blocks, as well as Jordan almonds. So the women made their own dessert, smashing dried figs with sugar and oil and dusting the mixture with crushed and sugared garbanzos. And when they cooked, they cooked together — rolled grape leaves or zucchini and tomatoes baked in earthenware.

She knocked on the door of her dead grandfather's house — Attiyeh. Oh, he was beautiful. So beautiful they called him the German — blue-eyed and white-skinned and very tall. He loved women. And they loved him. To visit his mistresses, he would wear women's clothes and sneak into their houses. Until he was discovered. He escaped by jumping out of the window and taking off his women's clothing. His fear caused him to fall asleep on the mountainside, his clothes under his head like a pillow. The Ghoul found him, and the shock of seeing her paralyzed his mouth and tongue for a very long time. Much later, a married man with grandchildren, he would take Afaf to Jerusalem; while he prayed the Friday prayer at the mosque, she would go to Bab Al-'Amoud, one of the ancient gates of the city of Jerusalem, marvel at its towers, and jump down its ancient steps to buy the green furry almonds she loved and that came in brown paper bags and salt for dipping.

She knocked on the door of her dead grandmother's house — Rasmiyyeh. Rasmiyyeh's *thobe*, like those of all the women, was sixteen meters long. When she wore it, she would fold it over once, tie it with a belt, and then fold it over again so that the second layer became a huge sack attached to the body — an 'ib. She would pick her vegetables and fruits — her murreira, her khubeizeh, her olives, her peaches — and carry them in her 'ib — like a built-in basket, always there, always ready. Once, one of the women, after a long day at the fields, found a snake in her *'ib* when she opened it up to lay it out across the room. When it needed to be washed, the *thobe* took the length of the entire line as it dried. Her grandmother swore that she would often walk and see chicks and chickens and that she would carry them in her *'ib*. But when she returned home, they would disappear; they were djinn, a *rassad*.

She knocked on the door of her dead cousin Widadeh — the only cousin to "west" in her marriage. All the other women married from within the tribe except Widadeh. On a visit to her family from the neighboring village where she now lived, she passed out. The doctor ran his fingers up and down her soles and declared her dead. All the other cousins ripped their *thobes*, jumped up and down in unholdable grief, blackened their teeth with dirt, slapped their faces with agony, and sat around her body in a circle, singing sad songs. They walked behind her body for miles to the cemetery — the entire tribe — hundreds and hundreds of people. They buried her in the *fusqiyeh*, the family's mausoleum. She was buried with the others whose bodies had turned to bone. Years later, when they buried someone else with her, they found her skeleton in a seated position.

She knocked on the door of her dead mother, Sabha. Together they had cooked on the *babbour* and used it to warm themselves on cold nights. They would gather themselves under the quilt and lift it up so that the flames from the *babbour* would not lick the flammable fabric and set them alight.

She knocked on the doors of her living cousins and reminisced with them about all the weddings they attended. The bride would wash her hair with the water jug and homemade soap (from olive oil). And they would cover her face and escort her as she was carried on her horse to the groom's house — half a mile up and down the hills. Her family would be behind her, singing and clapping, bemoaning her leaving even though she was going right next door: *She left her parent's house and left her sister and has gone.* And celebrating the beauty of the groom: *His neck is two palm spans above his shirt; our groom has passed through our neighborhood. The perfume is on the jacket, the suit is from Kuwait, the bride is his, so put perfume on his jacket.* The family would announce the marriage with lit torches so that people in the neighboring villages would know there was a wedding; for seven days, the men would sing and clap and friends would come to visit from all around. The torches called to them, told them there was happiness here, in Al-Mukaber Mountain. Told them that there would be tea with cinnamon, cooked in a huge cauldron, and enough for hundreds. Told them that there would be no homemade desserts here, only the best sweets brought from Jerusalem, filling the large trays. The women would grab the sweets by the fistful and throw them at the crowded guests — whoever caught, caught, like a bird catches rice.

She knocked on the door of her living cousin Zareefeh and asked her to sing to her again all the songs she knew. The ones for weddings. The ones for mourning. The ones for circumcision. The ones for pilgrimage. The ones for birth and death. Zareefeh is the only one who remembers all of them. When she dies, that door to memory will be shut forever.

She knocked on the doors of her old elementary school — a simple structure of three rooms, two grades in each room; she and her cousins would travel to it in delicate groups — *zarafat.*

And some doors she could not knock on. Some relatives she could not visit. A portion of her neighborhood, called Sheik Sae'ed, is now bisected, severed from the rest of the mount by the "wall."[5] A visit there would take too long. A trip that, before the wall, would have taken only minutes.

Oh, to truly be a specter who could fly over walls or a sound that could travel, like a bird, from one house across the valley to another, calling on your kin to come for breakfast.

———

As a child in Palestine, Afaf wanted nothing of houses and their doors. The children had to be persuaded to go inside; they preferred to spend the whole day and the whole night outside, playing marbles, five stones, and hopscotch. Jumping on the stones in the valley, provoking — and trying to avoid — the little snakes poking through.

But now all she wants is to be welcomed back into those houses and through those doors. So many of them she knew, and so many of them new to her. With nine paternal and three maternal aunts, each having raised ten children who each had ten children of their own, there are hundreds of houses and doors unsouled from her. She knocked on them with her hand, real, not spectral.

When she left Palestine in 1967, Afaf says that though she tried, she could never find her soul again. And that in exile, as it would in death, her soul had left her, returning only on that visit — like a bird who had finally returned to its nest.

And then it stayed for forty days and bid its soul goodbye. Again.

Blaise, from Burundi

Blaise was born in Burundi in 1988, though his ID says otherwise.

"When were you born?" I asked him.

"What do you mean?" he said. *Is there another way to ask this question?* I wondered.

Sensing my confusion, he quickly added: "Which birth do you mean: the ID one, or the real one?"

He was *really* born in 1988, but the refugee resettlement agency mistakenly added four years to his age. This mistake is bigger than the more intentional error I have noticed over the years. Many refugees whose birth certificates are incomplete or not available are given a birth date of January 1 in the year of their birth, even when they themselves know the exact date.

Their knowing does not seem to matter.

At the dentist's office once — with the family of four from the Democratic Republic of Congo we were hosting on Guilford's campus at the time — the receptionist marveled at how all of them had the same birth date.

"What a strange coincidence," she said in her kind southern drawl.

I told her it was not real. It was a mistake. A date officials chose to make the process of resettlement easier.

I didn't tell her that birthdays are nebulous things — the real and the not real. That they mark different beginnings, including the one where someone decides that it is easier, better, more convenient to tell your story — to set it down — than to ask you.

Blaise was *really* born in 1988 into a family of five or six. He is not sure about the number, for he has been told that he has a brother, though he told me that he has not met him.

In the course of our conversations, this brother frequently came up. Blaise *has* met him, albeit under unusual circumstances.

He is an elusive memory, this brother. Everything before and after him is vivid, sharp, stable, set down. But this brother is both there and not there — like a twin to Blaise, his other self, only faceless.

Blaise is the last-born among his siblings. His oldest sister died when he was nine — not the one who raised him, who fought for him. That one — the sister who raised him — was the second-born. Her name is Flavia. She is his second mother. He loves her more than his guitar. More than his parents, who died very young of a disease.

Blaise said straightforwardly, as if it were as easy as a January 1 birthday: "All of them were sick. Just simple. They get sick and then they die." His father died one year after his mother. She was thirty-six; he was thirty-nine. And Blaise was six, and then he was seven.

His parents were mixed — his mother Burundian and Rwandan, and his father Burundian and Congolese.

He caught their languages — Swahili, French, Kirundi, Kinyarwanda, and Lingala. When you are living a language, it is easy to catch.

Not like an infection, but like a strong wind in your open sails.

Blaise's mother tolerated everything. Like his father's concubine, whom one day the father abandoned, refusing to pay her rent or send her money or food. No one knew what went wrong between them — that story was not set down; it went with his father and mother to their graves. But the concubine was thrown out of her house. She gathered all of her belongings and placed them at the entrance of her lover's compound and waited there to confront him on his return from work.

In the compound, news of the gate watcher reached his mother.

"I heard that you are here for my husband. What is wrong?"

The concubine misheard a fight in her question.

"No, I did not come to fight. I just want to know," his mother said.

And so the mistress told her story — loved and abandoned, and then evicted.

His mother, Maria, upon hearing the story set down, decided to carry all of the concubine's belongings into the house — along with "the kid."

"The kid?" I asked.

"Yes, my brother. I don't remember him . . . But I remember his mother, Maria."

He and the other Maria's boy are the same age. People who saw them, knew them, set down their features in their minds, said they looked the same.

Born to two Marias and one handsome father.

———

The first Maria took the other in. Cared for her. Fed her. And in the face of the father's anger at the appearance of his concubine, the first Maria stood resolute, for this Maria never fought.

"You hid from me that you have a concubine. But now I have heard it." The story had set itself down. "Now sit yourself down; we have to fix this."

His father wailed. He did not want to see her or hear about her, this other — this second — Maria.

"And what about the kid?"

Leave him behind, the father said.

But the first Maria called her daughters, Blaise's sisters, and asked them to take out all their clothes from their room. In there, she set down the other — the second — Maria.

She stayed there for two years, when her family eventually came for her.

Later, when news of the first Maria's death reached her, the second Maria returned to care for her children as if they were her own. "Did she bring the other boy, your half brother, with her?"

Blaise doesn't remember. He can remember things before that, things after that. But not this boy — who looked like him and came from another Maria and his handsome father.

Some bodies, their memories, are hard to settle. And the power to set them down — to give them birth on the first day of the first month — is not one to which we ever feel entitled.

Yes, the first Maria tolerated everything — saint-like.

But truth be told, whenever Blaise has a problem, he misses his father, not his mother. On hearing that Blaise was bullied, for example, his father would have simply said: "What are we waiting for? Let's go fight." His mother, a devout and practicing Christian, would have simply said: "Go down on your knees and pray for that person."

Sometimes — many times — this is not the answer you want, even if it is the answer you need.

Sometimes — many times — you want someone to give you permission to fight.

Maria never did.

A Sunday school teacher, and a singer-songwriter in the choir, she had a beautiful voice. Blaise can remember the songs she taught him, but he can't remember the exactness of her voice. Like his brother — he knows her voice was there, indelibly making its mark on him, but he can't set down its contours, see the features of its face, hear it, conjure it. But it has set itself down, without his trying: Like her, he became a singer and a songwriter, his music inspired by the gospel sounds he heard at church with his mother.

But Maria's soul wasn't initially what settled in him. As an orphaned child, living with his uncles in the Congo after his parents' death, he was treated badly, outcast in the dark shadow of their passing. His anger grew; as a teenager it infected his body. He worked on that body incessantly, honing its muscles that longed to fight. And he fought with everybody, even his uncles, even strangers on the side of the road when there was no one else to fight. When he fought with a soldier who was about to arrest his friend and became wanted for a year until the intervention of an army friend, Blaise knew it was time to change.

The body needed to reunite with its set-down story.

Maria's son needed to find his purpose.

"Go talk to God," mother Maria used to say to her son whenever the hours between those conversations stretched too long. Blaise remembers that command more than anything else.

He returned from Congo to Burundi and became a worship leader in a congregation of five thousand people. His church is the mother church — the church that gives birth to nearly all the churches in and around Bujumbura, to nearly all of the preachers of the city and its suburbs. One of its shining sons, Blaise was tasked by the mother church to grow a burgeoning congregation of fifteen people. He was given a period of two years to raise them up.

Blaise was animated by the challenge: If one comes into a church, and it is already big, what is the challenge there? But what happens if one goes into a small church and *takes it up*, creates it? Within two years, the congregation grew to six hundred. This sprouting from a humble seedling is Blaise's greatest achievement, especially because his young church represented the "new wave" — where there were none of the fractures Blaise witnessed at the larger, older churches: the invisible, bodiless fight between the generations; the older not wanting to be replaced, the younger wanting to replace them. They did not put their hands on each other, but you could hear it in the way they talked to each other.

On the day of his departure to the US — a Sunday — his congregants gathered that last afternoon to bid him farewell. They cried and confessed to him that they had found their way there, to this smallest of sprouting seedlings, after hearing Blaise sing the songs inspired by Maria's soul.

"I was far away. I heard your voice. And so I came."

"Usually," Blaise says, "the people you love, you start to miss them once you turn your back. Once you say goodbye. That is when you miss them.

"But I started to miss them before I even said goodbye."

After the last gathering at the church, Blaise took the International Organization of Migration (IOM)[6] bus by himself to the airport. He had not expected to see anyone there. But there they were, at least thirty of his congregants. The airport's three domes loomed over them, as if a church had sprouted up then and there where they all were. In their last moments together, they asked him when he would be back.

His answer was simple: If it was all about him, it would be tomorrow.

"I love you. I don't want to spend three days where you are not. But it is not all about me."

And he waved his soul goodbye.

Cheps, from Uganda

Cheps was born in Uganda in 1990. His mother died when he was five years old. His father had other women — two or three perhaps. And so his grandmother raised him in her lap, in her small house. She was the best of women. And life was good with her.

In Sabiny, she would tell him *chatianguet* — stories, prose poems of lessons meant to build up his life.

Sometime in the before — a long, long time ago — all the people would gather together and drink and tell stories about their wealth. One man would say, "I have my cow"; another, "my four bulls"; and yet another, "I have my farm." One day, a man who had no wealth wanted to be part of the boasting: "I have a hen that always wakes me up in the morning." One of the members present *you-you*'d and made fun of him. "No one wants to hear about your hen. What are you talking about? People are talking about cows, and bulls, and farms, and you are talking about your hen." The shamed man kept quiet. He was a poor man who had wanted to feel that he too possessed something that meant something. A something unto which he could gaze and say, "This is something big in my life." And so he kept quiet, quit the group, and went to sleep. In the morning, he got up, carried his spear, and walked over to the house of the man who said his hen was too small in the face of all the cows, the bulls, and the farms. At the door of the belittler's house, he asked the wife: "Is your husband still here?" "Yes," the wife replied, "he is still sleeping." And so he walked in and killed him in his sleep — piercing him with his spear until its tip met the ground underneath.

"Look to the words that come out of your mouth," his grandmother would say. "Watch them. At the time, they might look good to you. You may like those words, your friends may like them, but the person you are talking to, their soul might be a stranger to you — you never know what kind of person they are. Be with your friends, but learn how to speak. It will help you in life."

Another story Cheps remembers is familiar to me; I had heard it many times from my own grandmother in Jordan. You need to make sure that a goat, a lion, and sweet potato leaves cross the river safely, intact, so you can carry no more than two across at a time — the two where one would not eat the other.

In my grandmother's version, the animals and the greens are different — a coyote instead of a lion, a sheep instead of a goat, grass instead of sweet potato leaves. They make sense to the Levantine lands we lived in, their flora and fauna, just as Cheps's grandmother's version was true to East Africa.

But the lesson is the same. Some things cannot be left alone together, just like some things cannot be said. Relationships can be tenuous, dangerous; but they need not always be fatal if they are managed carefully.

Cheps carried these lessons with him. Be cautious, they told him. Watch your mouth and watch who you're alone with — a wrong word or a wrong pairing can mean your death or the death of others you love.

Cheps was thirteen when his grandmother passed away. She missed his circumcision ceremony, but she had made him resilient enough for that rite of passage.

He stood with all the other boys in the village — all of them fourteen years of age or so — dancing. They were given no painkillers, only a whistle to blow when the deed was done. The strength to blow the whistle at the moment of excruciating pain, he got from being raised by his grandmother. But there is a gentleness, a kindness there, too, in the community that made this bearable. The whistle is meant to be a response to the call sung by the watchful men and women. When they sing the call, the boys ought not to reply with words. How could they, when they are in so much pain? Instead of a scream, they whistle, to relieve their pain, to pierce the sky with it all the way to the heaven above.

The older men's call is meant to deliberately egg the boys on — their words designed to infuriate them so they can be distracted, strong enough to endure the burning pain to come.

"You will die alone!"

Whistle.

But then they lift you up: "You will be a man!"

Whistle.

This is a test to check the mind, Cheps says. How the boy reacts tells the community how he might handle the harder things of this world. If he can pass this pain, then the community and the boy himself know that he will succeed in life, that he can cross to the other side without being eaten, that instead of words said in the heat of the moment, he knows now to depend on a careful response that pierces the sky and not the heart.

The men's last call requires no response. In the morning, the elders welcome the young boys home: *Hhhehe serod kumugana.* "Welcome back our lovely children. You are most welcome back. Now you are going to be real men."

Before the circumcision ceremony, the families of the boys gathered all their friends, their family members, their neighbors, the distant relatives who came from afar, and they danced the whole week, and all the night before. The community gathered again the next morning to watch the boys become men. Their pain is not suffered privately, individually. The pain is public, shared, collective, carried. It is witnessed and appreciated. And the gravity of its role is not lost on Cheps. The man who circumcised him — Cheps knows that this was his role in life, his purpose. There are strict rules this man also needed to follow. For example, if he ever must circumcise a boy who had passed (and who must not be buried in the earth uncircumcised), he can never go back to cutting the living. He is a lion turned into a goat. He cannot be in the boat with the tender sweet potato leaves again.

After this rite of passage, the boys now have the right to say to their fathers: "Father. I am a man. I need a piece of land. And I need a house to start using my life."

Cheps's father gave him a piece of land.

And now Cheps is building a house with the little money he sends back, on this very land in Uganda, for the little boy, his little soul, that he left behind. He knows that one day, his son will come to him and say, "Father. I am a man. I need a piece of land. I need to set up my life. What have you left me? What land have you given me? What house have you given me to use my life?"

And he cannot let his son live a life unused.

But this right to use one's life — to make it one's own — comes at a price. It must be done the community's way. No other way. Even the boys who join the army to avoid being circumcised. The community watches for them. One day, they come home, and all of the men of the village are there. Waiting. It is a simple choice: "Do you want to die or do you want to be circumcised?"

Cheps thought he had done enough to be part of the community. To stay alive in it and for it. Until its laws made his soul a stranger to theirs.

In the community, relationships are delicate, tenuous, dangerous, and must be managed carefully. And even though the community accepted Cheps when he was fourteen, that did not mean that they would accept him later in life. In fact, the community will deem him no longer a real man. No longer welcome back.

The goat turned into a lion.

Marwa, from Iraq

Marwa was born in Baghdad in 1986. As an infant, she was so soundless that her grandmother who raised her would forget she was even there. One time, at court for the marriage of Marwa's uncle, her grandparents were startled by her presence. They had simply forgotten they brought her with them.

Her mother worked. Her father, in and out of work, stayed home more often. And so her memories are mostly of her maternal grandparents' house. Marwa remembers how her aging grandmother would struggle on walking trips. Stopping frequently to sit down, her grandmother would declare, call out loud, her last will and testament: "Marwa, I entrust to you your mother!"

Her grandmother's frequent stops to rest her body — on sidewalks, on benches, on chairs outside shops — were mistaken for the norm by one of her grandsons, who always walked with her. Whenever he traveled with anyone else, he would walk and stop, walk and stop, sit on the sidewalks, the benches, the chairs outside the shops as if this was how people always walked.

But even though her grandmother's body aged, her hair did not. Until the day she died, she had only a few strands of gray. Marwa would count them, marvel at their luster and the scent of bay leaf soap, the only soap her grandmother used. Sitting at her back, Marwa, with her little hands, would comb and braid her grandmother's bay-leafed hair. And whenever her grandmother put henna in it, she would also spread some of the thick dye on Marwa's soles and palms and make her sleep on the rooftop, the wayward dye too powerful to trust on delicate indoor bedding.

When Marwa's wedding day was nigh, a relative died. Her grandmother insisted that the wedding should be postponed, for weddings ought not to happen too close to mourning. Marwa's family insisted on moving forward with the wedding, but her beloved grandmother refused to attend. It took Marwa years to find the courage to look at her wedding pictures and videos; they had reminded her of the beloved's stark absence. Her grandmother's anger did not last long. She came to visit her as soon as she heard that Marwa was pregnant, fearing that her granddaughter's sadness and tears would feed the growing baby in her belly. Unable to walk by this point, Marwa's grandmother dragged herself to the upper rooms where Marwa lived in her in-laws' house and crawled down afterward like an injured cat. On her visit, she entrusted Marwa: "Do not sit too long facing your dark father-in-law lest your child be born in his image!"

The day before her death, she asked for Marwa, but Marwa could not find someone to drive her there. She missed her grandmother's last rites as her grandmother had missed her wedding.

One day, Marwa's sister-in-law came to visit her in her rooms upstairs. "It smells like your grandmother's house." How happy that made Marwa. Her grandmother's soul had blown bay leaf and henna in the night sky air, and they had settled in her room.

Marwa remembers the soul of her grandfather's house. Her grandfather was a world traveler, and in their visiting room, the special one where only the guests were allowed, he kept the marks of his travels: the delicate china from Thailand, the painted large seashells from Russia, the peacock feathers from Turkey displayed in a vase, as if they were flower stems. And he kept the marks of his numerous friendships, the wedding favors — still unopened — chocolates and Jordan almonds and delicate flowers in transparent rectangular boxes. But she and her siblings were beloved, and they could come in and out of the room unchecked — banging the seashells in pots, sniffing the peacock feathers, and washing the delicate wedding favor boxes, opening her own mother's: a delicate purple dentelle filled with candy, the sweets inside still delicious years later. Back then, someone took the time to create those favors, to fill them gently, to tie the delicate napkin.

And Marwa untied, opened, and ate with abandon.

How different this abandon, this access from her paternal grandfather's visiting room that was never opened to them. Marwa
watched it from afar. The books, the statues, the stuffed animals —
a wild red fox with a bullet scar in his body and dead beady eyes.

Her maternal grandfather was a farmer who loved animals, and
though they always died, he would buy new ones at Suq Al-Ghazel,
the Friday animal market. Every week, he would buy a new crea-
ture to care for. When his children were little, he was appointed
to a village for a period of time to help the farmers there learn
new techniques in farming. His mother and unmarried sisters held
sway over him and his family; they made the decisions about who
ate and what, and who went to school and where. So whenever his
wife, Marwa's grandmother, birthed a son, they would take him to
"be raised well in Baghdad." Three boys all told. Her grandmother
would have the chance to visit her sons on the weekends. Their
childhood pictures told a strange story — the boys are elegant,
city-clad in their elegant suits. The girls are villagers, simply garbed
in tattered clothing.

To this day, the siblings shame each other: "I was raised in the
city; you in the village."

All in Baghdad later on, the grandfather with those same sons
would frequently visit the banks of the river Dijla. Marwa's
grandfather would set her on the bank, the *jurf*, and swim back
and forth, cutting the river once, twice, three times. Not knowing how to swim, she would watch the men's arms slice through
the waters, a watermelon cooling in the lapping waves next to
them. Exhausted, the men would come out, cut open the red
fruit cooled by Dijla, and the children would eat, drowning in
its sweetness.

Marwa's grandfather died when she was twelve years old,
but his kindness was legendary. Even though he spent a year in

bed completely paralyzed after his stroke, none of his children complained about having to care for him. It was as if they were caring for their own limbs, their own bodies, their own souls. And when he died, they mourned him as if he had died suddenly, healthy, not slowly, burdeningly so that the hour of departure was longed for.

They say that good people suffer greatly before their death. God wants to shed them of their sins before he meets them.

An interesting oxymoron, I thought. If they were good, how do they have so many sins?

As if reading my thoughts Marwa mused: "Maybe he wasn't that good."

To let that happen to his wife. How hard it is to take a child away from their mother. And in an assassination attempt on his life, the shrapnel hit her grandmother, pregnant at the time with Marwa's mother.

"Yes, maybe he wasn't that good to everybody all the time."

But Marwa knew that she loved him, so much that she never used a single gift he had given her; she would simply take those out and look at them, filling her soul with his, cleansed of all its sins.

Relationships are tenuous. They must be managed carefully, lest one break them.

One day, after a big fight between her mother and father, her mother proclaimed that she would be leaving, that she would go to her family's house — *tihrad*. This is an experience unique to Arab women, where the woman deliberately, intentionally packs her bags and goes to the house of her parents — her keepers. There she waits for her husband to come get her after he has righted the wrongs that drove her there in the first place.

But Marwa's father didn't follow. Instead he immediately sold his wife's sewing machine — the expensive Singer. He took the money and spent it on the children on a trip to Samarra — the city so beautiful, it brings joy to those who lay their eyes upon it. They ate at a fancy hotel, swam in the lake, climbed up the spiraling tower of the ancient mosque that looked like a desert cake. Through it all — the eating, the swimming, the climbing — Marwa cried. Her dad, incensed, yelled at her that he had done everything for her; this trip was to make her happy. Upon their return, they found her mother at home, having changed her mind. Instead of going to her parents, she had gone to her in-laws, to *his* parents' house, hoping that would make it easier for him to make that trip of appeasement, that simple gesture of love she wanted him to make, softened by her decision to protect his pride — only his parents instead of hers would have to witness her retrieval.

Her father might have intended to make them happy, to forget her mother's angry departure. But all Marwa could think about throughout this trip was how they took something her mother loved and sold it to buy them a few hours of joy in a city that pleases the eye.

Yes, the men are good. But maybe they aren't good to everybody all the time.

Ali, from Iraq

Ali was born in Baghdad in 1971. He is the second of six children — two boys and four girls.

His childhood was wonderful, made more wonderful by the women in his life.

Like his "milk teacher" in kindergarten. She was so beautiful, Ali drank the milk she handed out to the children even though he hated it. Her beauty overcame him so that he asked his father to exchange her for his mother. His heart broke when she was gone the next year.

Like his neighbor Amna. As a baby, he would wake up early — the first to open his eyes in the house, driving his mother crazy

— and he would descend the stairs and crawl to the wall that separated them from the neighbor's and call to her: "Anna, Anna." Hearing him on the other side of the wall, Amna would ululate as if her groom had arrived, and his mother would lift him over the wall to hand him over to Amna's family. They would play with him all day — ululating and clapping and singing as if he were a husband, handed over from his family to his bride's to spend the day. When Amna got married, Ali was so heartbroken he cried during the entire ceremony. He refused to take a picture with her, in her beautiful white dress, when she asked him to. A five-year-old lover betrayed.

Like his youngest aunt, Ibtisam, who lived with them and was raised by Ali's father, her brother. She took him with her everywhere she went — to visit friends, to attend vocational school, to shop at the market, even to clean him in the shower. At night, he slept next to her. When she didn't take him on her service trip — instituted by Saddam for youth to build affordable houses during their summer vacations — and took his older brother instead, his heart was broken. He could not stand being parted from her for that long. A seven-year-old best friend betrayed.

Like his grandmother, who in the long tradition of Iraqis (before the war changed the very air and made the trees less frequent than the buildings) would sleep next to him on the roof in the summer. She always came down to sleep indoors in September when the nights were too cold for summer sleeping but warm enough for the gentle fanning of the *mahaffa* — the fan made from palm leaves by the women of the house. The stationary roof beds — made of metal and painted to withstand the winter weather — were set up in rows, a bed for each family member. Every night, they were decked with mattresses and pillows brought up from the house. Ali's family had so many members, their roof looked like a barracks — with extra beds for summer guests. As soon as the sun set, his grandmother would call him so that together they could spray water on the roof floor to cool it down. By the time the family went to sleep, the beds would be so wet and dewy, they felt cold. He would sleep with his grandmother and aunt on the upper roof, elevated above the lower roof, where the rest of the family slept, by a flight of stairs. His grandmother's dawn sounds usually woke him — drinking and gurgling with the water from her jug (*qulla*) — making her ablutions for the dawn prayer.

Like his mother, who knew and memorized all of the traditional songs sung to children — the songs about Eid, the songs about playing in the streets, the songs about marriage, the songs about birth, the songs about leaving your family, and the songs especially for girls, and the songs especially for boys, for one cannot spin the beauty of boys and girls in the same way, in the same song.

The midwife brought me the news that I birthed a girl. May a snake bite the midwife.

The midwife brought me the news that I birthed a boy. May she visit the sanctuary of the imam.

The midwife brought me the news that I birthed a girl. May the midwife receive a hoard of gifts.

The midwife brought me the news that I birthed a boy. May the midwife receive a hoard of bones.

Oh my children, wait until he grows — strong and straight and standing. Oh wait, until we dress him in his wedding garb and give him to his bride. Ali, my son, you buy, but not for us. You will send them to your beloved and forget about your mother and sisters. Ali, my son, you work but not for us. You will send them to your beloved and abandon your mother and sisters.

Ali, recognizing how precious this memory is — for he knows that when she dies, all of that memory would die with her — transcribed all of these songs. Now they cannot be forgotten, cannot be erased, can never die. And now, Ali works, buys, but never just for his beloved. He sends to his mother and sister. He will never abandon the other women in his life.

Like many of us, Ali played in the streets until dark: marbles, soccer, matching cards, yo-yo, and bikes. He and the neighborhood children played *the house of houses*: pretending to be adults, married, living a life with children, making decisions about love and discipline and work and doctors and meals.

Like many of us, Ali loved playing in the neighbors' garden: well cared for by the grandmother who lived there. She tended carefully to the roses she planted, its row of orange trees, its ceiling of vines, its one large narenj tree. Those fruits marked the end of their dinners in the summer — the jarnek, the grapes, the watermelon, the narenj. They would watch the children's programming on TV (the Arabic *Sesame Street*) and then go to sleep in Iraq's starlit nights. In bed by eight.

Like many of us, he helped his parents with the household chores: harvesting the two olive trees — green and red — for his mother to pickle after she poked them with a fork and submerged them in salted water. The trees' lower branches, he would pick from the ground. The higher branches, he would have to climb. And the farthest ones, the unreachables, he would tap with a stick to persuade them to let go of their fruit. His family harvested enough to be able to give to their neighbors who didn't have olive trees — the neighbors who had roses, and vines, and oranges and narenj for juicing. While all the neighbors had their own gardens, their own paradise, each had their distinct fruit that they would share with the neighbors who didn't have that particular tree come fruiting time. His family gave the olives. In return, they got dates and mulberries.

Like many of us, Ali sat at a big table during lunchtime at school. Along with his friends, he would make fun of the other children, like the Iraqi boy whose mother tied his sandwiches with string so they wouldn't crumble and fall apart and the Palestinian girl who ate a strange dark-green bread, which Ali would learn later was za'tar. Back then — when the sectarianism that wreaked havoc across Iraq didn't yet exist — the most Ali knew about difference was children turning up their noses at foods they didn't have at home.

Yes, human bodies on the move don't always take their souls with them.

Sometimes, they leave their souls behind. Their aunts and grand-mothers, the living and the dead. The sisters who raised them. The communities that once loved them, gave them the strength to whistle, sharp and strong, in the face of pain. The bay leaf–scented rooms and hennaed beddings. The watermelons cooled by city rivers. The wet, dewy roofs and olive trees with fruit enough for everyone, including the neighbors.

When refugees leave, it is rarely, if ever, happy. And it is never something they choose to do.

Their bodies, finding no other way to survive, split themselves from their souls, wave goodbye to them, on the fragile hope that soon, they will meet again.

3

PROOF AND PERSECUTION

Refugees leave their souls behind and strike out — on planes or cars or boats or foot — to cross borders they must cross to keep themselves and their children safe.

Like a flock of birds, a school of fish, a dancing crowd, a mass of dead bodies, refugees are entangled in their perceived sameness. But they are all different. Their stories are different, and so are their experiences of persecution that have caused them to flee the homes they loved, their souls — to solve the problem of death with exile.

Anybody can become a refugee.

Most refugees never imagined that this is who they would become. Indeed, my own family became refugees quite unexpectedly. In 1967, a week before the expansion of the Israeli occupation that displaced thousands of Palestinians, my mother, uncle, and grandmother went to join relatives who were visiting Jordan at the time. In 1967, one week before the Israeli incursion into Palestine, the distance between the White Mountain in Jordan and Al-Mukaber Mountain in Palestine was less than an hour — an easy day trip. Now it takes days, the travelers intercepted by checkpoints, and bridges, and roadblocks, and the Jordanian government, and the Israeli occupation. But this was a week before the '67 incursion, when my grandmother took her children and decided to go for a short visit — and never returned.

Before Sabha left Al-Mukaber Mountain and walked across the river Jordan, she decided to pass by her brother's house. They waved each other goodbye — she from the street, he from his front door. There was no need for elaborate farewells, this would be a short visit. As she walked away, she turned her head and jokingly sang to him: *My greetings and peace to you, oh people of the Occupied Territories.*

This was a song they had heard frequently on the airwaves: Palestinians sending their love and support to kin who were separated from them in 1948. Their bodies unable to touch, they would send their souls in songs, lamentations, and impassioned lengthy greetings that in occupied homes emanated from static-charged small black boxes. The kin would huddle around the radio, waiting for the sounds of an uncle or a cousin calling them out by name: "My greetings to my cousins Suha and Rana and Widad in Yafa, and my respect to my cousin Yaser and my uncle Amin languishing in Israeli prison."

And so jokingly, she sang on her way out: *My greetings and peace to you, oh people of the Occupied Territories.*

Little did she know that one week later, this song would invoke the truth — a persecution now expanded — and that her entire tribe, the family she left behind, would now be occupied. Little did she know that a week later, her nephew would have his intestines spill out in front of his mother and aunts, her sisters, when a cannon hit him in the stomach. They tried to put the intestines back in, scooping them with frantic hands, but he still died. The aunts and uncles and cousins left behind in Jabal Al-Mukaber had heard such horrors of Israeli soldiers, and they all scattered in the mountains, fearing the rape and the murder that was to follow. Hiding in the caves, they drank water with the livestock.

Sabha and her children stayed as refugees in the camps of Jordan, unable to cross the border they had crossed a week before in one hour. It would take my mother fifty-five years to cross all the way back, the bird to its nest, the soul to its body, the spectral hand knocking on the doors, wondering who was still there — alive — behind them.

———

When refugees become refugees, the pain of persecution followed by the pain of fracture and departure is often amplified by the burden of proof placed on refugees. To be recognized as a refugee eligible for support and resettlement in a third country,[1] the fact of persecution is not enough. The phrase *well-founded fear* in the United Nations High Commissioner for Refugees' (UNHCR) definition of a refugee is a serious one that is taken very seriously. It means numerous interviews and interrogations — by the local government of the country to which one has initially fled, then the UNHCR, then the refugee resettlement agency, then the embassy of the country of resettlement, and then, if chosen to be resettled to the US, background checks by US Homeland Security.[2]

Every agency needs their interview, their interrogation, their pound of flesh.

When I started working with refugees in 2016, I had not known about this particular requirement — the repeated screening interviews, which necessitate the repeated, unchanging, identical narration of the "origin story" of why one became a refugee. When we hosted our first Syrian family on Guilford College's campus, I went in those early days of our friendship to visit them. I sat down for tea with the mother, Um Fihmi, in their spacious living room facing the woods. I had come casually — in the way of Arabs — and I can't remember what I asked. It was a simple question — polite, harmless — something like "How are you doing?" I know now that questions about one's being, when asked of a refugee, are never simple. Their experiences have taught them that such questions are a test upon which their very futures, their very safety, their very being — about which I was seemingly harmlessly asking — depends.

"How are you doing?"

Um Fihmi's answer came quickly, easily, and at length — a perfect, flawless, rehearsed, and deeply painful and intimate origin story: the beautiful building in Homs, the plans for more levels on top for the other sons about to get married, then the darkness, the neighbors slaughtered, including the toddlers and the infants, their throats slit, the fear that it was the other neighbors who had done it. She had recognized his voice under the mask when he came around that day, threatening; he used to come over for tea, in the *before* days, unmasked and gunless. Then a gas canister exploded in the house; she came out, "blackened," and unthinkingly cursed Bashar. The neighbor heard her. She tried to cover up what she said but knew their days were numbered. The next day forty men came, masked, and threatened to kill her entire family. They tried to take her youngest son, Tamer, then ten, because they said he had been at a protest against Bashar. Under the cover of night, they gathered themselves — so many of them (all the sons, all the daughters, all of their husbands and wives and children) — and fled. Along the way, a very long journey, they were almost run off the roads by highway bandits, hid in bombed-out buildings, nearly lost a baby when, in the chaos of an explosion, everybody scattered and her daughter gave her granddaughter quickly to someone else. They found the baby the next day, taken care of. But many other children, the children and grandchildren of others, including her own siblings' children and grandchildren, were not so lucky. At the end of her recitation, she kept saying that while it was hard, they made it with their honor intact. So many women had been raped. They had narrowly escaped that and were so proud and grateful that they had. "What we have tasted, no one has tasted," she told me.

At the time, this origin story seemed to come out of nowhere, an unasked-for explanation, a justification that was never demanded. Only later, when I found out about the repeated proof of misery required of refugees in the claims assessment process, did I understand. My question and the dynamic of our relationship — I, a service provider, she, a seeker of safety at our doors, a recipient of our benefaction — the need for our support, the fear of it being taken away, triggered that recitation, that soliloquy on the stage of refugeedom: a trauma constantly triggered and retriggered by the refugee admission and resettlement process.

All refugees have lived lives that are distinct and individual — complicated, rich, layered. Something happens in their lives that fractures them from their souls, their homes. A fracture that threatens their safety. And it is a fracture they are not allowed to forget. Their future depends on forever remembering their persecution.

Blaise

In 1993, when the civil war erupted in Burundi, Blaise's father decided to escape, take his family back to his home country of Congo. There they thought they would be safe from the death — the machetes that shone, by moonlight or sunlight, as they struck, sliced through, brought down by arms that looked just like their neighbors', their own. *Had they too, like Um Fihmi's neighbors, come over for a visit in the before days?*

But in Congo, death followed, silent and viral. First his mother, saint-like, and then his father, handsome. Blaise had just enough time with them to catch their languages and his mother's songs. He still had his oldest sister, he thought. But soon after their father's death, she died too, at sixteen.

The earth under his feet scorched again — this time in Congo — just like it did in Burundi, burning itself, its trees turning on its bushes. And so in 1996, his second-oldest sister, Flavia, decided to go back to Burundi — the scorching there less recent, the scent of burnt buildings and bodies less pungent. She took Blaise with her. She didn't have to. Young herself and without a support system, Flavia didn't have to fight for him. Could have left him behind. But she didn't. She decided she would raise him as if she were his mother, as if he were her son — unseparated by scorching wars.

And unseparated by a husband and children of her own, so that even when Flavia married and returned to Congo for her husband's work with her own child, she took Blaise with her.

In Congo, the land had not enough time to cool before it burned hot again, and in 2002, Blaise and his second mother, Flavia, this time with her husband and child, gathered their disparate selves, bid their souls goodbye, and fled, yet again, to Burundi.

Wherever he went after his mother and father's death, Blaise says, he was not safe.[3]

It is this last persecution upon which Blaise's refugee status is based. When his family (his sister, brother-in-law, and their young child) fled Congo, they tried to cross the border amid intense shooting. Their first attempt at crossing was by land, where they were stopped by rebels.

The rebels made them all kneel. And Blaise, at thirteen, found himself in the face of a gun barrel.

It would not be the last time.

The rebels let them keep their lives but took everything else — their clothes, their money, their papers. And with no papers, Blaise and his sister and her family could no longer cross the land border. So they headed for the river — a small offshoot of the Ruzizi that separates Congo from Burundi: the Kahorohoro.

Blaise remembers that it was nighttime and pitch black. This particular river is treacherous, dangerous, muddy, and filled with sleeping hippos and watchful crocodiles. Blaise realized, as he was about to cross the river whose waters could never put out the fire of the burning earth, that his last conversation with God was too, too long ago. And so he prayed. "Keep the hippos and the crocodiles where they are," he beseeched. "Do not let them sense our presence. Do not let our paths cross. Please, do not let my skin feel their smoothness, only the muddy waters."

They emerged safely on the other side, soaking wet, and slept under a tree all night, weighted, set down.

Now safely in Burundi, they applied for refugee status with the Burundian government. Blaise was only thirteen, and as a minor his case was included in his sister and brother-in-law's as he was considered part of their family. His brother-in-law and sister, the representatives of the family's case, told their story of persecution to the Burundian government.

And then they told it again, and again, and again. To the UNHCR, to the refugee resettlement agency, to the IOM.

Blaise thinks frequently about this part of his refugee journey. The officials, the interviewers who walked into the room. The first time, they brought with them empty sheets of paper that left the room filled. Filled with Blaise's set-down story.

After that, in every subsequent interview, the officials, the interviewers, brought with them those papers, the no-longer-empty-but-filled-papers where he first spoke his pain out loud, shortly after the harrowing escape — from the barrel of a gun against his lowered head, so low because he was kneeling, and from the muddy waters of the river, so muddied with hungry hippos and clamping crocodiles.

There it is, *that* story. They would ask him questions, and they were expecting to *read*, exactly, word for word, in his spoken answers, the story that had already been set down when he was thirteen.

In the process of becoming a bona fide refugee, the set-down story becomes the person, and the person has to be a faithful representation, narration, of that set-down story. The interviewers tried to trip him up, to test him, to push him to make a mistake so that he would deviate from his set-down story.

Blaise was initially interviewed when he was thirteen years old; the gunpowder and the muddied water's scent had barely left his nostrils. He believes that while the interviewers knew that he might not remember all the important details — he couldn't name certain addresses or certain places — he was too young to know how to lie about the important details: the facts of the case that brought them here, what they had witnessed that made them run for their lives. They needed him to corroborate, or not, his sister and brother-in-law's version of events.

When they interviewed him again at thirty (it had taken seventeen years for his case to be processed), he was still a clear reflection of the set-down story. Unlike other children who live non-refugee lives, Blaise's mind was not allowed to forget, not allowed to protect him from the pain; its trauma was written both in invisible ink on his body and in legible handwriting on the paper, *that* one the interviewer was holding in his hand, with his set-down story on it. His sister and brother-in-law's nightly drills, playing the role of the UNHCR officer, testing, pushing, tripping him up, all of it made sure that he would never forget.

"I think this was good, Diya." I could not see how.

Neither could he . . . at that time. But now he does.

"It taught me how to tell my story."

Because their case took so long, as those things do, when Blaise turned eighteen the UNHCR "chose to separate" him from his sister and brother-in-law's case.[4]

This happens more often than not — parents and children, siblings, their lives and deaths tied together, their fates and everydays intertwined in ways many of us cannot imagine, become separated from each other in the heaven of refuge by the passage of time and the rules that say what time means to familial bonds. Blaise and his sister were supposed to be together forever. Indeed, Blaise's brother--in-law was like a father to him; even though making ends meet was grueling, for he had no regular job in Burundi and the mouths of his own children to feed, his brother-in-law never once tired of

Blaise, managing to pay for schooling and, sometimes, a little something for Blaise to spend on himself because he knew what boys' lives could be like. And Flavia was his second mother. She fought for his life, took him with her and refused to leave him to the burning earth and machetes in Congo; she raised him, made sure that he ate, drank, lived. She loved him more than her own children, bought him gifts — even when he was a grown man — so he would not feel separated from her family. So that they would all feel equal.

When her children complained about this love, she responded with the ease of inseparable cases: "Of course. We have the same blood. What do you expect?"

But the same blood means nothing to the passage of time and the set-down rules that determine what time means to familial bonds.

Blaise got on a plane at an airport that looks like a church, and his sister, his second mother, stayed behind. Her case is still pending, pending.

"Why were you separated?" I asked. I wondered whether anyone explained.

"They don't explain themselves and their reasons," Blaise said.

Cheps

Cheps belongs to a community within a community. But really, it is a community *outside* of a community. One community is defined by its ethnicity. And it is at odds with the other community, defined by its sexuality.

One day, the bigger community realized that he, Cheps, was a problem.

"They call it a problem," Cheps says, "but they see it as something that does not even exist, that is not real."

But his beatings and torture were real enough. And it was real enough for the many other young people he knew.[5]

"Uganda is big," Cheps says. "And if I were any other kind of refugee, I would have tried to go somewhere else in Uganda. To be a refugee in my own country."

He tells me about IDPs: internally displaced peoples. "I know," I tell him. There are many Palestinian IDPs, including the millions who live, trapped, in Gaza and the West Bank.[6] IDPs remain in the country of their persecution — simply moving to another city, another region to escape the violence.

Yes, Cheps agrees, there are cases where one can be a refugee in one's own country, but sexual orientation is too big, too serious. It is bigger and more serious than other cases. Even one's larger community cannot accept it. Everywhere and anywhere he could go in Uganda, he would "not stand."

They would fell him.

Everywhere and anywhere he could go in Uganda, he would not be "used."

Cheps wants what all humans want. To stand. To use his life.

To stand, to avoid being felled, Cheps had to leave Uganda. And Kenya was right across the border where he lived in Suam. A friend who was working with a human rights organization advised him to cross the border and seek asylum in Kenya.

He crossed the border easily, simply. In fact, he just walked. He did not have a passport, but he did not need one to cross. Unless one has luggage, no one will check for papers at this very small border. They assume people are just going over for the day and coming back. And Cheps had no luggage. He was planning not to return.

But Cheps was carrying his faith, he says. An invisible small package he carried with him to a church his friend gave him directions to. Associated with Catholic Relief Services — the international arm of Catholic Charities — the church provides support to asylum seekers and refugees. Upon his arrival, he did not find the man he was supposed to talk to — the father. And with no money to sleep anywhere else, he laid his head on his small invisible package of faith all night.

The next day, he met the father, who advised him to go to Kakuma, one of the oldest and largest refugee camps in Kenya, and one of the most notorious refugee camps in the world. In exis tence for generations, Kakuma is its own system, its own culture, its own city. There lives the Turkana, a local tribe well known for their hatred of and cruelty toward homosexuals. They have no mercy. For them, the killing of members of the LGBTQ community should happen immediately. On the spot.

The lion with the goat.

But Cheps had no options. He knew that Kakuma would only be temporary. And after that, he would need to go to Nairobi.

Cheps spent the next three years in Kakuma.

When Cheps eventually reached Nairobi, he had to tell his story to the UN official.

In those interviews, Cheps's grandmother's lessons worked — he looked to his words, knew what to say, watched them as they came out of his mouth. The people who interviewed him were strangers to his soul. Within four years, his case was processed. Three of them were spent in Kakuma. One in Nairobi. His roommate, Marcel,[7] however, remains in Kakuma, eight years later. Marcel asks friends who have resettled for the money he needs to buy some water cans and some seeds to plant his garden in the camp. He stayed behind because he did not know how to defend himself in those interviews. In the boat with that lion, he was the goat. In the interviews, when they asked Cheps about his private life, prodding him to prove his case, he bit down on his dignity, clamped it down so that he could tell them what was painful, shameful, hard for him to say. Where was the whistle now, so that instead of the words, too hard to say, he can simply breathe out his response to their call? For others like Marcel, who is elderly and interrogated by a young woman asking questions about his most private life, it is hard to set down one's story, to answer the probing, direct questions, to lay oneself bare before a stranger to one's soul. Marcel goes back again and again, hoping, waiting, wishing that the next time he goes, the interviewer will be older, with gray hair like him, and maybe, just maybe, a member of the LGBTQ community with whom he can use the whistle instead of the words that catch in his throat and refuse to come out.

Marwa

When I ask Marwa about the war, she says, "Which one?" There have been many in Iraq, and each one its own separate misery, its own separate beast, but each one connected to the next in ways inextricable, in ways that brought her here to Greensboro.[8]

Marwa is diligent about memory. She knows that she was only four years old during the first war in her lifetime, the one that took her uncle. He was conscripted in the army and drafted for battle and never returned. His mother, her paternal grandmother, lived on the hope that he was alive in an Iranian prison or that he was an amnesiac, married and living a life somewhere in Iran, and that one day he would remember them and return. The fortune-tellers told her so. She kept his bed, changed its sheets, wouldn't let anyone touch his things. Watched breathlessly as through the decades meals of Iraqi prisoners were exchanged with Iranian ones. They had a system back then. The families of the missing would seek out the released prisoners, gone so long their faces were unrecognizable to their own families, and ask them to recognize the face of their loved one — someone they might have seen, known, perhaps shared a cell with, perhaps saw in the prison yard. Twenty-two years later a released prisoner captured in the same battle recognized her uncle.

"Yes, I saw him, shot, facedown."

He swore on the Qur'an that he was telling the truth. Her uncle hadn't even made it to prison. He died during the first days of the war. And there they were, thinking he was alive for more than two decades while his body rotted, dissolved, disappeared — dust in the wind.

Marwa is diligent about memory. She knows that her memories of that war are really just other people's memories, their testimonies, their witnessing. The strange look on her grandmother's face whenever prisoners were released, the relief that he was never found, and the relief that she died before they found out that for the past twenty years they were looking for, waiting for, dust in the wind.

Marwa is diligent about memory. She remembers that under the siege imposed on Iraq because of the war, they went hungry. Her mother's salary lasted until the middle of the month if they were lucky and only bought vegetables and grains, not meat. The schools had no windows; they were hot in the summer and freezing in the winter. If the teacher was able and kind, she would bring a small heater and put it in the room so the kids wouldn't stutter and shudder while they studied.

Her grandfather died under siege and from the siege. He was a child of plenty. And under the siege, he had to sell his house, all of those beautiful things in that magical room — the plates from Thailand, the peacock feathers from Turkey, the seashells from Russia — one after the other. He sold them in the market where you could sell anything and everything for nothing. He sold her grandmother's amber, goatskin rugs, the copper from Egypt. Yes, he was standing up. But he wasn't really. His eyes were always red. He ate his pain . . . until he fell. The slow and painful divestment of his life, in the slow piecemeal sale of one memory after another, struck and paralyzed him. He could not carry what happened, especially after he saw how his children lived and how his brother's nine orphaned children lived.

Marwa is diligent about memory, and so she says that she must not have been afraid because back then, she was too young to understand what bombs and rockets were and what an explosion does to a building and how it sounds.

But in 2003, she was seventeen. Old enough to remember how the sound of the rocket, when it fell, seemed impossibly close, like it was headed just for her, for the very spot on which she was standing. But it never arrived. It landed farther away, headed for some other family, on the spot another girl stood.

It went quickly, that war: The Americans first bombed the infra-structure. The country was paralyzed; no one could communicate or share information. Even the sirens trying desperately to warn, their wail was always too late, well after the aircraft had seared their space and dropped its load.

People left their houses and headed out of the cities for safety. When her aunt left her apartment, she put a Qur'an in the door to fend off whoever was breaking in — as if they would see the holy book and check themselves, be shamed, prevented from robbing, looting, vandalizing.

Her brother-in-law, who had just defended his master's thesis a few days earlier, saw someone steal his graduation robe and dance around in it.

All they could do was blockade the doors with the hope of other people's belief in their goodness and their shame in witnessing how far they might have sunk.

Without water and electricity, Marwa's family ate potatoes for a long time, the only thing they could safely store. The news claimed Iraqi victory; the Iranian channels told a different story. The Americans were already there, as was the fear from rumors of torture and rape. Her relatives bought weapons for when the police and army would inevitably disband and the dirty wars started.

Each neighborhood formed an armed band to patrol and protect its streets. But from whom? Everyone and anyone now could have been an enemy. On the rooftop with her aunt who was in the Party, they huddled as they burned her books about the revolution. Under the Iraqi sky, high up, they felt safe from the eyes of someone, a neighbor perhaps, who could seem one thing but turn out to be another. "But," they wondered, "if an American jet fighter flies overhead, can it see us? And if it does, will it bomb us off the face of the earth?"

It took them a long time to come back to Baghdad. That trip from her parents' house back to the city was a mourning procession. The side of the road was littered with burnt-out Iraqi tanks, the bowels of hospitals and schools carved out and eviscerated, broken computers, museum artifacts and statues, books. The animals at the zoo, with no one there to care for them, died slowly of hunger and thirst; the zookeepers replaced them with dogs so that there would be some kind of creatures in the cages. And her mother walked them to school carrying a knife.

There used to be a life in Iraq, but it got canceled, and something else, some other kind of life, came to replace it.

In June 2014, that other life took yet another dangerous turn. Marwa had been shopping for Eid clothes for her children. She hadn't known, like her mother had, that everyone woke up that day to Mosul being consumed by Da'esh, the radical fundamentalist militia known more commonly in the US as the Islamic State or ISIS (Islamic State of Iraq and Syria).[*] One after another, the cities fell. Her husband applied for asylum because the family could not

---

[*] Many Muslims and others call the group Da'esh, denying them legitimacy as a state or as a representative of Islam.

bear it anymore, the terror of the trucks, *again*, filled with armed young men, presumably gangs resisting Da'esh. The dirty wars alive and well a decade later. They were surrounded by people fighting one another, and like all similarly dirty wars, it wasn't clear who was who, and who was fighting who, and what they were fighting for.

In the silence of the night, she would sit on her bed and nurse her youngest, Yousef, and watch the gangs (her balcony overlooking theirs) in the building next door. They had taken it over and were massing there. Marwa would wonder, vulnerable in that house, *Can they make that jump from their balcony to mine if they wanted to? Can they kill me and my children? They have taken over homes, lands, farms. Will ours be next?*

And why not her next?

Everything else was being erased. History, culture, mosques, museums — drilled, exploded, destroyed. The world called this a liberation, but it was really an evisceration, an erasure. And the country no longer felt like her country. Moving from one province, one district, one city to the next was a leap of faith, that the gangs that would stop them would be from their sect and wouldn't shoot them in the head, right then after looking at their IDs. One time, she and her husband and infant boy were en route to visit her parents where Al-Qaida was in control; they were stopped by bandits whose faces were covered. The car driver had already made his peace, had told them that he was not responsible for any passengers.

The disclaimer for lost lives as casual as the disclaimer for lost luggage.

She prayed hard. There with Ali in front and little Abboudi in her lap. When they asked the men for their IDs, she turned her face in anticipation of the kill. Ali's name looks like it's from a sect that is opposed to theirs. Ali begged them to call his uncle, a man well known in the neighborhood. They let them go. She walked into her parents' house yellow-faced, every drop of blood drained. She refused to go back to that house until Al-Qaida left, a liberation as equally painful as the siege.

"If this is no longer my country, can this be my home?" Marwa wondered.

And then home became even more dangerous. While she was visiting her parents, Ali, her husband, left as usual for work at 5:00 A.M. On his quiet walk to the car, a bomb exploded nearby. He spent the next three days in the hospital in critical condition. During her visits to the hospital, Ali would comb through his hair with his fingers and remove the pieces of shrapnel his skull had ejected. The rest, the ones un-ejected and the ones too dangerous to remove, have settled to live there, skin tissue growing over them. She learned how to treat him at home and learned more about how human flesh reacts, collects, and dies than she ever wants to know again.

Yes, death is everywhere; she knew that. But she felt it close to her then. Too close.

Ali

Ali loved Iraq. Leaving was not something he had ever dreamed of, and coming to the US had never occurred to him. Indeed, after a few years of living and working in Jordan, "westing" was something he decided he would never consider. And this was after living in a country that was similar to his own — the food, the language, the culture. But exile tasted bitter, and Ali did not want that taste in his mouth again. So he returned to Iraq to get married and settle for life. And it was a reasonable dream. After the fall of the Iraqi government, America promised that Iraq would be stable now. Resource-rich, Iraq had every chance of giving its sons and daughters a promising future.

But the dreams turned into nightmares: sectarianism, chaos, and corruption slowly ate away at the country's riches and its dreams of stability. When Mosul fell to Da'esh, Ali knew this would be the end of his sense of safety. He lived in constant fear for his wife, his children, and his own life. He looked around and saw that everybody who could do so was leaving — the doctors, the professors, the engineers. And he decided to do the same. But for him, it was harder. Without sufficient finances or resources to leave, he would have to find another way, like those desperate to leave by any means necessary. But he knew enough of those who'd left by entrusting their lives to smugglers and had never completed the perilous journeys. He had heard enough and seen enough of the countless refugees who had drowned at sea in capsized boats and rafts, asphyxiated in the cargo holds of otherwise seaworthy and roadworthy vessels, succumbed to the limitations of their bodies, the elements, and the relentless indifference, if not cruelty, of the watching and waiting human race.

Ali had not known, until a chance visit from a former supervisor, that as someone who worked with the American forces in Iraq, he could qualify for asylum.

In the late 2000s, Ali worked a very brief time for an American company that provided maintenance for Iraqi vehicles. He typeset schedules, created stamps, and designed business cards. He didn't last long in that job. People working with such companies, even if marginally, were constantly threatened and attacked.

Ali, marginally, survived two assassination attempts.

The first time, he had been on his way to work while Marwa and their children slept soundly at her parents' home. He casually walked past a fridge on the street, on his usual route to his parked car. He absentmindedly noted its presence without surprise: There was always litter, even that big, on the streets of Baghdad in those days — the city always disemboweling itself. The bomb left for him in a fridge exploded behind him, when he was just a few meters ahead. Had it exploded sooner, had he been closer, he would have been killed. But he was just out of bounds for death. He heard the explosion first and then felt a stinging heat slurp at his back. Shrapnel from the fridge fiercely kissed him in his back, head, and bottom. He spent days in the hospital. They removed what they could of the shrapnel — the pieces visibly sticking out — and deflated the hot air caught in his lungs, suffocating him. To do so, they had to insert a tube through his side to let out the air as if he were an overblown balloon.

The second time he had been on his way back from work. The first assassination attempt had made him constantly vigilant, suspicious, on the alert about who was in the street with him, behind him, ahead of him — who was walking where and how far away from him. It was this hypervigilance that saved him. On this relatively quiet road, he immediately noticed the car behind him — driving too fast, as if hell-bent on getting something done and out of the way. As soon as he turned to look at the car, he saw the driver stick out his hand. Ali instantly dove. Had he been a few seconds too late in his reaction, he would have been killed. Had his fear not consumed him, he would not have turned just in time to see the hand, to see the gun, just in time to dive, just in time for the bullet to catch him in the leg and not the chest. Bleeding and in pain, Ali called his brothers to take him home. The spot where the bullet hit him is gnarly and fleshy now because he was too scared to go to the hospital, where he believed he would be exposing himself to more attacks. And so he treated himself at home. The gnarly flesh slowly healed — gnarly and fleshy.

And then Ali quit that job.

Years later, his previous supervisor, a Ugandan man, visited Ali. When Ali confided in him his desire to leave, his supervisor simply said, "Why not apply for SIV? You would qualify. I would support your case." SIV cases usually take two years to process, and his supervisor had known others who applied and were granted asylum.

Unlike Blaise and Cheps, Ali was a candidate for a Special Immigrant Visa (SIV), and so his interviews were less intense. But they followed the same pattern of interrogation and confirmation. The application he submitted, complete with pictures of his shrapneled head and back, his gnarly leg, needed to be an accurate reflection of who he was when he walked into the US embassy in Baghdad to be interviewed by the consul. Because Ali was Muslim, they asked other questions too: "How many wives do you have? Is this your only one?"

While Ali's only wife, Marwa, initially agreed to join him in seeking asylum — the memory of the gnarly flesh, of the shrapnel sticking out, the thought of widowhood and fatherless children was with her strongly then — she began to hesitate during the long time it took to process the case. Others who had left before them to go to the US, like their neighbor, had told them what life would be like in the US, and it wasn't easy. Ali wondered: Could he not be content, like the many millions of other Iraqis, to stay where he was? Could he not just live with the living as they were living? Was he better than them to be leaving their shared hell, their shared heaven? By turns excited to leave for his children's future and afraid to leave for his love of country, Ali waited for his case to be processed and for fate to decide his destiny.

And fate decided when he was attacked by a gang in 2015. While Ali was driving his car, in his usually careful and slow way, a man crossed suddenly ahead of him, intentionally, as if wanting to be hit. Ali refused to stop for him. He knew this trick — the sudden but harmless impact makes the driver stop, and the gang members threaten him with telling the police about the accident unless he pays them. Ali kept driving, but he had underestimated the gang's persistence, their need for money, their cruelty. They followed him in two cars, chasing him down, ramming into his car, demanding that he stop. He decided to keep going. Initially he thought he would go back home, but he changed his mind when he realized that he would be leading them to his wife and children. And so he drove back to his work, where he knew the street would be busy and whatever they did to him would be witnessed by many. As soon as he arrived, they pulled him out of the car and attacked him, claiming to be government officials. Ali was afraid of opposing them, of letting them know that he knew who they really were. When they grew more violent in their attacks, punching him and kicking him as he lay on the ground, passersby and business owners started to congregate. And when the onlookers began to intervene and pointed out the street cameras, the gang disbanded and quietly withdrew.

Ali knew then, as did Marwa, that it was time to leave.

Ali told Marwa he was charmed. Hadn't he survived death hurled at him from fridges and cars?

Life in the US would be okay. They would make it. His hands would help him design a new chapter, set a new type, draw a new path.

Anybody can become a refugee. Most refugees never imagined that they would one day be refugees.

How could they know, at twelve years old, that the daily ten-minute walk with cousins to the school on the next hill, twittering, arms entwined, like a joyful flock of birds, would be severed by a high wall and rifles, and a short visit that usually takes an hour would take fifty-five years?

How could they know, at thirteen years old, that a relative would unwittingly witness a mass killing and that the whole family would have to flee, swimming close together like a terrified school of fish, and be severed from their home by a small river?

How could they know, at fourteen years old, that being welcomed into the community, enfolded into its whistling comfort, was conditional and that the whistle offered protection and inclusion only as long as their breath exhaled the sounds of the communal song? Now with a siren at their back, they are severed from home by a border that doesn't even require passports and laws that would cut them down as soon as their own people laid eyes on them.

How could they know, at seventeen, that the cities so beautiful they pleased the eyes of whoever saw them, the statues and buildings older than generational memory, could be crushed to dust overnight, so pockmarked with bombs that their legs and pillars could no longer hold them up? Crumpled, they are severed from their history by a faceless terror with cannons and machine guns.

How could they know, at forty, that shrapnel would kiss their head, bullets would hug their thighs, fire would caress their back, and make them finally realize that next time, their country's love might be fatal. They are severed from their own loyalty to their home by the fear that they might not be alive in it.

Yes, anybody can become a refugee. Most refugees never imagined that they would one day be refugees.

4

RIGHT NEXT DOOR

Less than 1 percent of the world's refugees are ever resettled. The majority of refugees remain, sometimes for generations, in camps a bomb-sound away from the towns they fled, across a relatively recently created national border.

As an undergraduate at Yarmouk University in the north of Jordan, I commuted every day from the capital Amman to the city of Irbid. When the bus leaves Amman, right after Sweileh, it descends sharply into a valley before it ascends on its way to the green mountains of Jerash and Ajlun. The valley is called Al-Baq'a, and it is one of the largest Palestinian refugee camps in Jordan.

Of course, I had known about this camp all my life, but my every-day view of it — the daily descent and then ascent on the way there and back home — cemented in my mind the at once seemingly central (it is located on a major thoroughfare) and separate (it is a city unto itself) existence of Palestinian refugees in Jordan. Al-Baq'a Camp was created as an emergency camp in 1968 to absorb the Palestinian refugees displaced by the war of 1967. Initially consisting of five thousand tents hastily set up to host nearly thirty thousand human bodies, it still stands decades later. The tents have morphed into a shantytown's stiflingly close zinc-roofed rooms, prefabricated homes, and homemade, more durable cement structures. Narrow alleyways, too narrow for cars in some places, separate the homes. More than 100,000 Palestinians (according to UNRWA*) — or 128,586 (according to the Jordanian government†), or 200,000

* The United Nations Relief and Works Agency for Palestine Refugees in the Near East.
† "Baqa'a Camp, Palestinian Refugee Camps in Jordan," Department of Palestinian Affairs, http://dpa.gov.jo/AR/ListDetails/.

(according to local estimates from 1999[*]) — live in this area of half
a square mile. For reference, I currently live in Greensboro, North
Carolina, a city of 300,000 people in an area of 134 square miles.
Al-Baq'a refugee camp is more densely populated than the most
densely populated city in the world, Mumbai (76,790 per square
mile).

 Al-Baq'a means "spot" or "stain" — a place on the landscape
differentiated from what is around it in some way, some shape,
some color. For the passersby, and myself those four years I spent
hovering atop it on the bridged highway in a bus, it is the smell.
Both from within the camp, and from the olive presses surrounding it, Al-Baq'a emanates and is surrounded by a smell that is
powerful and rancid. Once, our bus was delayed over the bridge
for a while. By the end, the smell had disappeared. And I realized
that I just got used to it. It took only a matter of minutes.

Ninety-nine percent of refugees stay in camps, but camps don't
always look like camps. Like Al-Baq'a, what might start out as a
hastily set-up conglomeration of tents (for example, the often-
seen white ones with the UNHCR logo on them) evolves over time
into discrete cities with other cities growing around them as they
develop; they maintain their borders, porous though they may be,
of a people set apart — by their generational poverty, their smell.
And others, like Kakuma or Al-Zaatari, grow into cities hemmed
in by or cut off from the rest of the country, often on its very
periphery, close to its national borders. These are not so porous.
More like warehouses for human beings, or large prisons, their
borders are tightly defined, highly surveilled and securitized; one
cannot leave or enter without proper documentation. No longer
cities, they are countries within countries. Such camps develop

* Rnada Rafiq Farah, "Popular Memory and Reconstructions of Palestinian Identity:
Al-Baq'a Refugee Camp, Jordan," PhD dissertation, University of Toronto, 1999.

their own internal systems — political, economic, and social — a colony for ostracized people on the outskirts of civilization.[1]

When camps are first set up by the UN in collaboration with local authorities, it is done with the intention that they will be safe and supportive of civilian life; their goal is humanitarian. Achieving and maintaining this goal, however, has been a challenge as camps have developed their own gangs, armed groups, and political, economic, and sociocultural identities.

And some camps are not camps at all. According to the UN, many refugees live in urban settings. They live like specters, renting cheap and unsafe housing from local property owners, working under the table, and living a life of fourth-class residents since many of the countries they flee to already have their own second and third classes from previous wars and conflicts.

Ideally, the UN wants "durable" solutions for refugees, ones that lead either to a return to their country of origin or to successful resettlement in a host country; this means full integration and citizenship — true belonging.

Ninety-nine percent of refugees, however, exist in an unendurable limbo of prolonged duration in camps right next door to the countries they fled. Their children and their children's children are born there — the unimaginable length of time between their arrival and their never-departure transforms the absurdity of camp life into the norm of the everyday.

Afaf

Sabha's life was already hard when Al-Naksa of 1967 displaced her and many of her siblings. Completely illiterate, she was already abandoned by her husband and had two young children to raise.

And like the many Palestinians before them displaced by Al-Nakba of 1948, my grandmother and her two children lived in the refugee camp of Al-Zarqa'a, one of thirteen Palestinian refugee camps in Jordan located around the cities: Amman (the capital), Irbid, Ajlun, Madaba, Balqa, and Jerash (the largest Roman city intact outside of Italy).

In Jordan, they called my grandmother and mother "the displaced." Sabha would take her card — which showed her state of displacement and how many needed feeding in her family — and the UNRWA would give her sardine tins to size. A family meal just enough for its members. No extras for the cousins and aunts who might stop by unannounced, knocking on already-open doors. This was just as well. There were no cousins and no aunts and no open doors.

But Sabha would bring the sardine tins home and share them with many others just the same, the other Palestinian refugees who were their neighbors. Sometimes, she and her children would go days without eating, or just get by on bread and cheese.

Every day, Afaf would dream that she was back in Palestine. Following her soul, which she had left behind, her specter would travel by night, knocking on all the doors of all the aunts and all the uncles.

"I am Afaf. Open the door. Do you still remember me? I know we were meant to be gone only a few days. But we are now stuck here, displaced, forever."

In Al-Zarqa'a, they lived on White Mountain. Barren of any trees or life but for the coyotes and the scorpions that stung Afaf's brother, the desert of White Mountain was a far cry from the mossy hills of Al-Mukaber Mountain. Sabha and her children lived at the very top. To get there, they had to travel to the valley below by vehicle and then walk all the way up. From the two rooms made of mud and hay, Afaf could see the river — Seil Al-Zarqa'a. They called it a river, but this was because the Bedouins of this region had likely not seen true rivers before. What did they know of cool streams, of mossy hillsides, of wild thyme and mint? What they called a river was just a trickle.

Afaf would roll down the hill when she needed to get water for their drinking and cooking — a nasty-tasting liquid she suspected came from that dirty trickle she had to cross to get to school every day. At school, the other girls pulled at her braids, and the teachers threatened the refugee girls who misbehaved with the "Mouse Room," where mice would nibble at them.

Her mother decided to leave the camp and rent a small room in Al-Jofeh, whose houses were as dismal as the converted tent dwellings of Al-Baq'a. Their own home was so modest, its outhouse had nothing but a sackcloth for a door. Sabha fed her children by knitting loofahs and selling them for pennies each. Under the dim light of a Number 4 gas lamp, Afaf read all the books her father, now in Beirut studying at the American University, had left behind — Anees Mansoor, Taha Hussein, Naguib Mahfouz.*

The three of them, Sabha and her two children, kept moving, their poverty taking them from one place to another. They counted on the kindness of the other displaced, like Um Il-Ragheb's family, whose house was right next door and with whom they shared a wall. Whenever Um Il-Ragheb knocked on it, it meant an invitation to come over for a meal or to watch the TV Sabha did not have.†

They were living in Sweileh when Black September, a bloody conflict between Jordanians and Palestinians, happened.² Again, they depended on the kindness of neighbors. Their landlord, a Jordanian military man, hid them in his house downstairs when a cannon made a hole right in the middle of their living room and missed them by a body's length. They hid, terrified, having heard of the ways in which Palestinians were being slaughtered

* They moved with her, those books, into her married home, and I read them all when I was her age, in the same country, decades later. The children of the children of the displaced.
† My mother was able to buy a TV for her family with the meager stipend she got from the University of Jordan; she had graduated first in her high school class and earned a scholarship and some spending money to attend the university.

in the camps — pregnant women stabbed, children killed right in
front of their mothers and fathers, people flattened with tanks — a
fantastical, unimaginable violence.

"What made them hate us like this, so very much? What made
the wretchedness grow in their hearts so suddenly?"

In Beirut, Afaf's father was living a different life. He had left her
mother when she was pregnant with her. Had told Sabha that
he needed to divorce her so that she could remarry. Before the
displacement, Afaf had lived for a while with him and with his
mother, her grandmother, in the most beautiful Parisian-like street
in Lebanon — Al-Hamra. Her father put her in a boarding school
where Afaf looked at the icons hung at the head of her bed — Mary
and Jesus — and went to church and thought she was Christian.
At night, she felt alone, soulless, and so she would call to the girl in
the bed next to her.

"Aida, can I hold your hand?"

And they would hold hands all through the night across the vast
expanse of the beds as Afaf watched the specters of the passing
cars on the wall and imagined herself walking, knocking on doors,
hoping to be remembered. Until her mother remembered her —
though I am sure she never forgot her — and insisted on taking her
children back with her to Palestine, refusing to marry so she could
maintain custody.

Now Afaf likes thinking back on this time in her life, in the
Parisian-like streets, and imagining that her childhood, instead
of one marked by sardine tins, and mud walls, and sackcloth-
partitioned outhouses, and cannon holes in walls, was this one
instead — that she was a princess in a boarding school who went
skating, and to the cinema, and swimming, and shopping. Who
was bathed in a tub with olive oil when she once fell into a bush of
cacti. Who, when lost in the streets, was asked: Who are you?

"I am my grandmother's daughter." And she was returned.

In Jordan, the rooms and the houses were strangers to her soul. And no matter how many times she said "I am Palestine's daughter," she was never returned. She stayed in Jordan. Forever.

Um Fihmi

Nearly a year after violence tore through Syria in the spring of 2011, pitting neighbor against neighbor,[3] Um Fihmi had had enough of death and fear when her own neighbors and many others she didn't know, masked and armed, came into her house and threatened to kill her entire family and take her youngest son. She had had enough when all her body could do was fall to the ground, paralyzed, her tongue tied.

She got up that night, temporarily untied herself from the chains of the trauma that gripped her, and gathered her entire family — her four adult daughters and their husbands and children; her three adult sons and their wives and children; her youngest son, Tamer, then eleven; and her husband. They gave the infants sedatives so they wouldn't cry and alert nearby rebels and militia and pressed their bodies through the barbed wire that separated Syria from Jordan. That May of 2012 they made it across the border after a harrowing escape and an even more harrowing journey with all of the family intact — their honor preserved, their hearts and minds broken.

Although they had to cross the border illegally — given the nature of their escape — they had to present themselves to the Jordanian army so as to be processed as refugees. This would allow them to receive benefits in Jordan and be eligible for resettlement. Once the army established that they had no relatives to go to in Jordan, they were released on "bail" to live in Madaba, a city south of Jordan's capital, Amman. Madaba is well known for its ancient church, which houses the oldest mosaic map (from the sixth century) of the Holy Land on its floor. Um Fihmi arrived in Jordan two months before the establishment of Al-Zaatari refugee camp; now home to nearly eighty thousand Syrian refugees, Al-Zaatari is one of the biggest refugee camps in the world.[4] But like many of the Syrian refugees who arrived prior to the creation of Al-Zaatari, Um Fihmi lived as an urban refugee in the cities of Jordan.

Um Fihmi lived in Madaba for four years, a life marked with humiliation. Wherever they walked, she said, wherever they went, they were verbally assaulted: "May your honor be tarnished. You have eaten our bread. Drunk our water. Taken our jobs."

Although their landlords were very decent people, many in the neighborhood, especially the young men idling in the streets, saw Um Fihmi's family and knew who they were and, finding no one else to blame for their own personal misery, threw their misery at the newcomers.

During those four years, Um Fihmi lived in a small two-room house. As did the rest of her children with their own families. They cashed the food coupons provided by the Jordanian government to pay their rent since work was sparse — occasional school-painting, construction, cleaning. Her youngest, Tamer, missed three years of schooling save some tutoring he received from volunteers. His first year, he was bullied, threatened, and attacked with razors. The other children who did not know that their own misery, their own poverty, was not because of the Syrian refugees sliced his neck and backpack. Her grandchildren who are still in Madaba are now illiterate — they cannot write their own names. And the coupons have dwindled. Her sons cash them all out for rent and nothing is left for food. Two of her grandchildren fainted. At the hospital, they were diagnosed with malnutrition.

One of her youngest grandchildren, Hazar (then five years old), was lying in the living room of her own small home in Madaba when the ceiling of her dilapidated rental collapsed on her. It broke her leg, or so they thought. With limited medical access for Syrian refugees and no financial resources, Hazar's leg was given a basic cast and she was returned home. She cried in agony for days until she was brought back in, and it was discovered that she had broken her pelvis, which was now healing, separated from the rest of her leg.[5]

In Madaba, not everyone is the same. There are always the children of the good, the halal, who appreciate the Syrians, know that they have come from under a war. But not everyone is like that.

Cheps

When Cheps finally made it to Kakuma, one of the most notorious refugee camps and the world's largest, he found a thriving LGBTQ community despite the hatred and the threats. Community members kept a low profile; they stayed within the larger community and joined existing gangs and groups, virtually undetected. But when a law passed back in their home country of Uganda, criminalizing homosexuality, community members in Kakuma, especially trans folks, began to affirm and celebrate their identities, publicly, in activism and resistance.[6]

But Kakuma is big and diverse and contains multitudes. Other inhabitants, including Somali, Sudanese, and Kenyan refugees, did not stand for this. And so, the UN and the local Kenyan authorities decided that the LGBTQ community needed to be moved from Kakuma to Nairobi for their own safety.

"But how did they think they could ever manage?" Cheps wondered. They would move one group of LGBTQ refugees and more would come. They kept coming. The Ugandan government thought that passing a law with serious consequences against LGBTQ individuals would curb their growing numbers. Of course, it did no such thing. It just made them more visible — an even easier target — and more likely to flee for their lives.

———

In Kakuma, Cheps had a small house where he could lay down his head. All the houses are the same in Kakuma — small zinc-roofed homes. Squares with mattresses and pillows.[7]

And he would also farm — okra, sucuma, mreire. In the morning, he would water his land. In the evening, he would do the same. He would sell his meager crop to help make do. Knowing who to get in the boat with, Cheps chose his plot of arid land next to a police station. They had a water hose he could easily use to water his vegetables, but he would also wash the officers' clothes. This favor would come in handy later, when a police officer would help him escape.

In Kakuma, he lived with an old friend, Marcel, also from the LGBTQ community. They would plant their land together. As he talks about his friend, whom he left behind, Cheps thinks of ways he can help Marcel. He will send some money so that Marcel can buy some seeds.

Marcel sends him frequent updates about their community in Kakuma, the parades, the comings and goings, the new folks who have joined.

Heeding his grandmother's advice has served Cheps well. Don't get in the boat with the lion. And Cheps knew that in Kakuma, he was in the den. His UN interview was supposed to take place in Kakuma, but the line of eligible refugees was long, and Cheps was feeling the lion's whiskers on his back. Would he be eaten before his turn in line came?

One day his police officer friend told him: "Go to Nairobi on your own. Do not wait for the UNHCR here to process your case. If you have any trouble along the way, call me." In Nairobi, the same UN was accepting emergency cases. In Nairobi, he would be safer — with the goat. So on the advice of his police officer friend, one whose clothes he used to wash, Cheps saved his money and carefully planned his escape.

He knew that as soon as one exited Kakuma, there would be a roadblock where they stop the bus, take everyone off, and check to see if they have travel documents or passports.

Refugees especially are not allowed to move anywhere in the country. They have designated places to stay like Kakuma, and any movement outside of those places must be sanctioned by the proper documentation. Cheps had none, and so he knew that he could not be on the bus as it encountered that roadblock, for he would be pulled off immediately and returned to the lion's den. He made a plan to catch the bus on its long trip on the stop *after* the roadblock. He bought his bus ticket and arranged for a motorcycle ride on the back roads from Kakuma to the bus's next stop.

He told the bus driver: "I will wait for you 'in front.'" Cheps took the off-road. He's on the boat now. The lion is on the other bank. Will he make it?

Cheps made it safely to the next stop after the roadblock, a small village where everybody knew everybody. He stood out, conspicuous, like a bunch of sweet potato leaves waiting to be eaten.

The locals saw him. Found him strange. One of the women came up to him and asked him bluntly: "You look like you are not from this community. And this is a very small tiny village. What are you doing here?"

Waiting for the bus.

"Waiting for the bus? Where are you from?"

Kakuma.

"That is where the buses are supposed to start from. Why do you come here to wait for the bus?"

The community leader joined the interrogation: "Here, we have a problem with terrorists. We believe you must be one of them unless you answer our questions. What are you doing here?"

Cheps is caught. Which one is worse — to be gay or to be a terrorist? He initially tries to be neither. He called the community leader aside, talking to him in Swahili. He tells him that he doesn't have an ID, that he cannot prove who he is, but he is not a terrorist. He is just passing through, hoping to make it to Nairobi. They insist that he is not telling the truth. And that if he has nothing to worry about, then they can just send him to the police station, and he can catch another bus there. But Cheps had already paid for his bus fare with the meager funds he had saved planting those vegetables. If he goes to the police station, he cannot buy another ticket, and the fare already paid will not be refunded.

Cheps realized he had simply gotten into another boat with another lion, and so he heeded his grandmother's advice. He moved whatever money he had left in his pocket — not enough to buy a ticket but enough to cross the boat — into the man's pocket and talked to him, as Cheps put it, "in a nice way." He watched the words coming out of his mouth carefully.

How gently one needs to speak with the lion. How calmly.

It worked. The men set him free, and Cheps got on the bus to Nairobi.

Finally in Nairobi, Cheps marked its size: "If you put Raleigh and Greensboro together," he told me, "still you cannot reach the bigness of Nairobi." All he had known of places in his lifetime was his small village in Uganda and the heavily regulated Kakuma — a large but easily navigable waiting room. Although the bus driver told him the name of the area where the UN offices were located, Cheps could not locate it. And at night, Nairobi was not safe for a stranger alone. When he saw some men sitting outside a building, talking and enjoying themselves, Cheps decided to ask them for help and directions.

But he found himself again in that deadly boat, not knowing which was better — to be the goat or the sweet potato leaves.

"We have a problem with terrorists in Kenya,"[8] accusing him, just like the villagers at the stop beyond the roadblock. And another interrogation began: "How are we going to accept what you are saying? Where are you from? Why are you going to the UN? We are worried about those UN officials. They are keeping the refugees in Kenya."

"Tell us everything. Exactly."

"What about the police station? Can you tell me where that is, please?" Cheps asked.

"We are now the police. Right here. Right now."

He knew that he was in trouble and that he could be killed there. *You are now in our hands*, they seemed to be saying, *and if you don't want to answer our questions, well then, your other choice is death.*

And so he had to tell them everything, and hope that being gay was less worthy of murder than being a terrorist — that for this lion, he was the sweet potato leaves, not the goat.

Their interrogation shifted once they heard who he really was. They humiliated him. Jeered at him. He was no longer a suspected terrorist, but a pariah, to be derided.

"Ah, you are the ones who are fleeing from Uganda to come here for shelter, right? Now tell us, how did you become a homosexual? And how do you *do* it, exactly? And why don't you think it's against the law? Don't you think it's unnatural?"

Cheps bit his lips and tried again. "I am gay. I was supposed to be killed just for that. But I am not a bad person. I am just like you."

In a nice way, Cheps explained. Moving a little bit of his pride, a little bit of his soul from his pockets to theirs.

The men finally let Cheps go after realizing that while he was not worth saving, he was not worth killing either. They directed him to the UN offices and warned him that it was best for him to spend the night outside the building, surrounded by security. And so he slept outside, on whatever invisible package of pride and faith he had left, under the falling rain. In the morning, the UN offices asked him for the travel document that all LGBTQ individuals coming from Kakuma had to have to show that their case was processed there initially. And when he could not show it, they told him that they would need to send him back. He decided to call a friend of his, another member of the LGBTQ community whose case was processed and who was leaving that day to his refugee resettlement destination. This friend had worked as a translator for the UN office in Nairobi and had connections there to whom he recommended Cheps. The officer whom the friend called ordered the security officers to let Cheps in, interviewed him quickly, and sent him to the HIAS (a refugee resettlement agency) safe house where they host refugees whose cases are being processed in Nairobi.

Cheps spent three days there, and with some financial assistance from HIAS (initially $120 a month, reduced to $60 after two months), he found an apartment along with four other men from the safe house. They pooled their finances to pay rent, feed themselves, and pay for the transportation to the frequent HIAS and UN interviews.

Cheps made sure he attended all of his many appointments without fail, taking on additional work as a barber to afford his transportation expenses.

He needed to get out of this boat and onto a plane as soon as possible.

Blaise

When Blaise applied for refugee status in Burundi in 2002, he first needed to register as a refugee with the government, which then submitted his name to the UNHCR. The government gives refugees a permit to be presented to police officers who might inquire about their status — who they are and what they are doing in the country.[9] The Burundi permit is a sheet of paper, a scarlet letter, a flag that screams out: *I don't belong here, but you have given me shelter, so please be kind to me.* It was too heavy for Blaise, this mark of otherness, so much so that he could not walk with it.

And so he didn't.

And Blaise was able to make this work because one could not take him out of the picture of Burundi.

If every country were a family photo album — flipping through its pages, there are faces we know and others we recognize as our ancestors because we look like them, and somehow, they all fit together, they are part of the same story — then Blaise fit right into the album of Burundi.

He spoke the language perfectly and knew the culture deeply. Indeed, Blaise could have applied for a Burundi ID because his mother was half Burundian, but he chose not to as this would have jeopardized his brother-in-law's (and hence sister's) case if he broke off from them and did something different. Refugee cases are incredibly precarious. The slightest change — in address, in marital status, in the number of family members, in residency — could thwart a case and take it off course for years, delaying its passage through the interminable pipeline. Blaise set down his story with his sister, his second mother, and did not deviate from her river.

In Burundi, they chose not to live in the refugee camp because his brother-in-law wanted to work as a teacher. And after they set down their story, they were released into the general population with a "Go, we will call you."

Blaise experienced war yet again as a refugee in Burundi. In 2015, now in his twenties and after almost thirteen years of living as an urban refugee,[10] Blaise faced the barrel of the gun once more. When the Burundi president wanted to be elected for a third term, the population rose against him in the quarter where Blaise lived. In their anger, his neighbors and friends took up arms and began fighting with the police and the army. But these were citizens who had no experience fighting. They retreated to their houses and shut their doors — hoping to see the next day — when the fighting got too intense, too complicated for them. But the government needed to find them, to eliminate them. Officials (both police and army) started knocking on doors, accusing families that their sons were involved, had shot at them. They gathered every young man from that quarter into one large group.

And Blaise got swept up in the madness. He was in the family album, part of the picture.

Hundreds of men were laid on the ground and the soldiers stood on their backs with guns to their heads. Threatening to shoot if they did not name names, oust their friends. Blaise swore he didn't know any names. The boy next to him was shot in the head. "It was a few meters of luck," Blaise says.

Had he been a few meters to his right, he would be dead.

That day, two hundred men were killed — men Blaise knew, had seen in their quarter, were part of the real family album. Not like him, an interloper, a pretender. But by chance, they left him.

They left him.

Blaise knew he could have taken up the gun too. Raised his fist.

But he remembered his mother's command. *Go, sing to God.* And in his church of five thousand, that is exactly what he did.

My heart is tired.
I feel as if I should lay everything down.
I have been on this journey far too long.
How am I still this far away?
My way is full of fog. I cannot take even one step.
I want to hold the promises I made, but my hands are too
*   short, and I cannot reach them.*

Ree Ree, from Burma (Myanmar) / Thailand

One does not always become a refugee. Many times, one is born a refugee.

Ree Ree was born a refugee — in Thailand's Tham Hin camp. Her parents fled Burma in 1997, the year Tham Hin was founded — built for people just like them, sprung up to receive them.

She's a year younger than that camp, born just as her parents got there. Their journey out of Burma was long and meandering. One of her older sisters — her mother was in the early days of pregnancy with her when they fled their village in Burma — was born in the jungle during the family's long flight.

Two more girls were born in the camp. The last sister, thirteen now, was born in the US.

When the Burmese soldiers attacked their village, they burned everything down to ashes, including her parents' marriage certificate and family photos. When her family left, they took nothing with them except the baby in their arms and the one in her mother's belly. During the day, they hid and slept. At night, they walked. It was on one of those nights that her sister was born — months after they started their journey.

By the time they got to the camp, her mother had another child in her belly — Ree Ree.

In the camp, the family initially slept on the dirt ground inside bambooed walls and plastic-tarped houses with logs for corners — something resembling a foundation. But over time, her parents, who were good at designing cut-down bamboo, made their house into a plastic-tarped castle with two stories and a balcony.

And her parents worked hard. Her mother never kept her hair long even though long hair was prized, a sign of beauty. What use had she for long hair? It was always too hot, anyway, and she couldn't do much or work as hard as she needed to with all that heaviness on her head.

———

At camp, Ree Ree went to school, like all the other children. Their efforts were put on display for all to see — their successes and their failures.

Life's expectations, the rituals of pride and shame, the daily concerns that mark everyday existence, transpose themselves to camp life, for life in the camp doesn't know any better. It doesn't pause to marvel at its own strangeness, doesn't falter to wallow in its own existential absurdity. Camp life sticks to its story that life in here is just like life out there. What matters out there, matters in here too. In short, life goes on.

And at Tham Hin, education was a matter of public concern. The logic of life there rejected the supposed temporariness, the emergency of camp life — and said simply: This is normal life, and here, we do normal things. So every year, the children's grades would be posted. This was fine until first grade, when Ree Ree's grades plummeted because she could not stand her teacher, a cruel woman who would hit the students if they did not study hard enough. The teacher had one unusually cruel form of punishment — when students didn't show up for a tutoring session, she would make them carry classmates on their backs and run five laps around the school.

Ree Ree did not want to be part of this punishment. Did not want to burden her peers in this way. When they rounded the building, out of sight, she would hop off her classmates' backs and, together, they would walk the rest of the way until they were in sight of their teacher again, when Ree Ree would hop back on.

I wanted to tell Ree Ree that maybe, like your mother, this person insisted on hard work because that was the only way to survive camp life — not only in the *now* where success and the insistence on it could make you feel like you were *somewhere else*, somewhere where success mattered, made a difference, led to something — but also because it was preparation for the time after leaving the camp, when people in the real world would not be gentle with you, or care, if you said, "But we lived in a camp, not the world. We lived in a camp where life stood still because we needed to reflect on its existential absurdity. We lived isolated and imprisoned. Be gentle with us now as we learn how to be in the world again."

Ree Ree left the camp before her teacher did. Now she is the commencement speaker at her college graduation. The first in her family to earn a college degree.

But at the time, even success succumbed to the absurd logic of camp life and its existence.

The students who earned the highest grades won a prize — water containers big enough for the family to store water and have all they needed for their meals that day without having to go frequently to the water source, carrying the water back and forth in their small jugs and pots, waking up early to get to the irrigation system that came on only three times a day, hoping they beat that one woman who rose earlier than the rest and hogged all of the water to herself. If they didn't, they would have to settle for the river water and boil it well before they cooked with it.

But Ree Ree was never afraid of the river water. That's not why she reveled in winning those prizes. Indeed, she would look into the river water, see the little mosquito larvae, tickling themselves, and would dip her face in and suck the water — the mosquitoes tickling themselves in her nostrils and mouth.

She enjoyed her ability to win things for her family to make their lives easier.

There was power in that. Control.

There was no control in being woken up early by the forced sweetness of her mother: "Hey, *puminchee*, it is bright and early! We still have an hour before school starts. The day is so nice. Why don't we go to the river before it gets messy?"

Ree Ree would fall for it — the playfulness, the love. She would carry her two jugs — a gallon each — to the river to help collect the water. Those would be brought back to be poured into one of the big jugs Ree Ree had won for her family.

She was six years old.

Ree Ree was a crier, and in those early years in the camp there were many restrictions.

LIGHTS OUT. NO SOUND.

But what do you do when a baby cries? When you need to be able to see to change its diaper, or feed it, or give it comfort and love?

Her mother did her best. Covered the cracks in the bamboo walls as much as possible so that candlelight would not send out its rays. But the neighbors were afraid. "Zari, do something about your daughter!" The camp banded together to move their family to a different side of the facility, a different district, farther away from the ears of the Thai government.

But Ree Ree's crying didn't stop. One day her older sister, so frustrated with Ree Ree's crying, threw her into a pond. The elderly neighbor next door fished her out. He was the only person who could calm her whenever she would cry.

"What did you do with my Salibeno?" That is how Ree Ree got her nickname: Salibeno.

Ree Ree, Salibeno, left the camp before he did.

At the camp, Ree Ree missed out on seeing what normal familial relationships look like. She believes that her current inability to be intimate with people is due to the strangeness of the dynamics that camp life created. She remembers the intimacy of cutting her grandmother's nails with scissors. When they fled, her grandmother was hit by a bullet that flew through her arm and cut her nerves. In her old age, she got so fussy they built her a separate hut. Ree Ree would cut her nails but refused to spend the night with her. Instead she wanted to play with her friends. These rejected snuggles haunt Ree Ree. When she broke a healthy tooth on a soft rambutan, she believed it happened because she had just lied to her grandfather about being able to spend time with him. Her chipped tooth sits there in her mouth, a sign of her rejection. Her failure. She wishes she could see him now, by the campfire, in his *teku*. Opening his legs and lifting his skirt to warm his body on those cold nights.

Camp life tries to be like real life. But it is not. It haunts and disfigures. It dismantles and distorts.

Tham Hin was highly securitized and surveilled. If someone was caught leaving the camp, they would be imprisoned (within the camp) unless they could pay the fine.

But every day, Ree Ree's parents would sneak out of the camp for work — a daily risk of being imprisoned in their already-established isolation.

They would leave before sunrise to cut down bamboo for selling and return after sunset. Her father liked the work, and he was good at it. But the daily heaviness cut down his back; he carries the pain of the bamboo's load to this day still.

Cutting down bamboo was illegal — yet another risk in addition to leaving the camp illegally. The bamboo wasn't theirs to cut. In the jungle outside the camp, it belonged to the Thai government.

Sometimes, Ree Ree would be asked to help with the daily cutting. She would drag the bamboo down the hill after it was cut, earning 5 baht for each bamboo tube she managed to bring down. Her small body averaged five heavy tubes every time she joined the work crew. Even though the work was hard, the 25 baht was worth it. She used it to buy the food she craved from Tham Hin's markets and at school.

On one of the trips, a section of the cut bamboo her father had secured was accidentally knocked down. He usually kept it straight, at a level where he could squat down to lift the individual tubes up on his shoulder. But the rock holding it up gave way, and the tubes fell on Ree Ree. Her little body pinned under the bamboo, she struggled to breathe as others frantically lifted the wood from her small seven-year-old body. Her dad pulled her out and shook her violently so she could start breathing again.

"A fond memory," Ree Ree jokingly says.

But there was something else underneath the wry laugh — "with the whole family, out in the woods, eating and being together.

"That's one thing I don't like about the United States. Trespassing. I am just taking a walk in the woods, and it happens to be your backyard. I am not trespassing, I am just breathing. You have nothing but your green grass. Not even bamboo."

Ree Ree remembers the support system at the camp lovingly. The girls who helped her, protected her from bullies; the man who tolerated her incessant crying in a place where crying was dangerous. The father who couldn't breathe when her breath stopped under a mountain of bamboo.

Ninety-nine percent of refugees never resettle. They live the rest of their lives, and their children live the rest of *their* lives, in camps or camp-like conditions in countries right next door.

Camp life is a rancid smell that hangs like a cloud on your everydays and becomes normal.

Camp life is an hour away. Is fifty-five years away.

Camp life is shared walls and shared sardines. Camp life is a cannon-sized hole in the wall and shared fears.

Camp life is a motorbike ride to the next bus stop and several nearly fatal interrogations away from real life.

Camp life is a war again, just like the one that brought you there.

Camp life is a man who tolerates crying when crying is dangerous. A father whose breath stops when his daughter's breath stops under a mountain of bamboo.

Camp life doesn't know any better. It doesn't pause to marvel at its own strangeness, doesn't falter to wallow in its own existential absurdity.

Camp life sticks to its story that life in here is just like life out there.

Camp life tries to be like real life. But it is not. It haunts and disfigures. It dismantles and distorts.

And the lucky less-than-1-percent carry their disparate selves yet again and strike out for lands unknown, hoping to find home.

5

BACK TO THE MARGINS

The lucky few who are to be resettled gather their disparate selves, say goodbye to their souls, and make the crossing one more time — this time not right next door, but thousands of miles away to a city they have never heard of, a place they have never known, a people they have never met.

Who will greet them at the airport? Where will they live? What will their new house look like? Where will they work?

Will anyone there speak their language, smell like their food, feel like home?

In January 2016, Cheps got out of the boat with the lion and onto a plane. Like every other refugee, he was asked to wear his IOM bag around his neck so as not to lose it. The ultimate signifier of refugees, the IOM bag is large, rectangular, white, and plastic. It is emblazoned with the blue IOM logo. For those in the know, it immediately identifies its holder as a refugee on their way to resettlement and contains all of the paperwork that defines their life. Cheps knew that the bag made him visible — even if he didn't speak English, even if he got lost, he would be found, for the white bag would call out his displacement, his status as someone on his way to find home. The IOM bag tethered him, like a lifeline, to his identity as a refugee to be resettled.

On the day of departure from Kenya, he and a group of other refugees — all marked with the IOM bag — started their journey from Nairobi to Tanzania, where another group of refugees joined them, including a family to be resettled in Greensboro. They traveled to Zurich and from there to Chicago. In Chicago it was snowing so much, all the planes were grounded and his flight to his final destination was delayed for four days.

Cheps knew nothing of Greensboro. In Chicago, he googled it. The rest of his friends who made it out of the boat had scattered around the world — to Canada, Australia, Switzerland. None of them chose where they would be resettled.[1] Their cases were handed off, and like dust in the wind, an invisible force determined where they would land.

Blaise had already swum in dark waters with hungry hippos and clamping crocodiles, lain under a soldier's boot with a gun to his head, been stripped of everything he owned by rebels. But nothing prepared him for the terror of the journey to his new home.

On a Friday in February 2019, he got the call that he would be leaving two days later.

"One builds a life," Blaise says. "No matter *how*, one builds it."

And the life he built would become his "legacy." It didn't matter what country he built this legacy in, it would be his very own all the same. In Burundi he had gotten accustomed to working out how to keep himself alive if a shooting broke out, a soldier put his boot on his back, screamed at him to call out the names, the bullet missing him by a few meters to his right.

But he was *not* accustomed to leaving his whole life behind in the span of two days.

He was not accustomed to leaving his second mother, who loves him more than her own children.

When one has been writing a chapter for thirty years, it is hard to receive the call that now, now, now, in two days, one must take up the pen and set down a new one.

Between getting everything done for the trip — the vaccinations, the paperwork, the orientation — Blaise was left with three hours to get his own personal affairs in order. Most of that time he spent saying goodbye. With no time to pack, Blaise got on a plane

that took him to Rwanda, then Ethiopia, then Dublin, and then to
Washington, DC, where it was so very cold.

On the last leg of the journey — to Greensboro — the plane
rocked so savagely that he held on tightly across the seemingly vast
distance of the airplane chairs to the person in the seat next to him
and imagined himself a specter singing to his congregation in the
small church he built up — his legacy.

Flavia, his second mother, waits for him in Burundi. She is also
imagining, singing in church, praying that her case stops being
pending, always pending, pending.

She is waiting for their set-down story to reunite her with Blaise
so that, together, they can write a new chapter. A chapter that will
be different, oh so different, from the one in ink on *that* paper that
keeps walking into their interviews and interrogations.

Ree Ree's father just wanted to go back to Burma — so that if his
back broke, it would be from working his own land, not illegally
chopping down bamboo to survive in temporary countries that
could never be his, that were not even a country — always on
the margins of made-up places and spaces that sprouted up and
entrenched themselves like shrapnel. So that if his legs needed
warming by the fire, and he needed to gently lift up his *teku*, it
would be around his family, the siblings he left behind in Burma
and those still displaced in Thailand, without citizenship.

But there was no going back to Burma. On the day Ree Ree's
family received notice of their resettlement, her father sent a letter
with others traveling through to his scattered siblings.

His letter was a simple message. It said: "We leave September
5th."

On September 5, 2006, as instructed by UNHCR, they waited at
the soccer field by the camp with whatever they could carry. The
field was a sea of people — the second cohort of Burmese refugees
from the camp to resettle in the US. Ree Ree was excited to get on

the bus until she saw her mother cry. At first she couldn't understand why, but then it dawned on her as the bus passed the multitudes, the faces she knew and loved, and then crossed the river and the faces were gone, gone now, gone forever. "I will never see those people ever again," Ree Ree realized.

The man who comforted her during her incessant crying. The teacher who tortured her. The woman who arrived early at the watering hole and hoarded all the water. The friends she scampered with, all in their underwear when it thundered and stormed, to play under the rain and in the mud. They would run to the church, its gutters funneling the rain, hard and forceful, its pressure delightful on their small heads. On the bus, she tried hard to remember because she wanted to make sure she could capture it all: The sound of the rain, heavy and hard; the specter of her companions' giggles; and the splashing in the beating shower — followed her all the way to Bangkok.

In Bangkok, Ree Ree's family spent the night at a hotel. It was Ree Ree's first time using a Western toilet and sleeping in a bed. Early the next day, the bus took their entire cohort to the airport. This large tribe of fifteen families — nearly one hundred people — got together on the same large plane to China. On the plane, Ree Ree didn't suffer from the motion sickness that struck the other Karenni families. While living at the camp, she and her family would sneak out to visit her mother and father's siblings who were scattered in different provinces all over Thailand. They would hop on an uncle's moped for a day of family fun in the city he lived in. This forbidden excursion happened only once or twice a year, but it was enough, those rides on the mopeds, on city buses and taxis, to prepare Ree Ree and her family for the plane ride. She watched in fear as everyone else spilled their guts, wretched and retching. Their lives in the camps had kept them stationary, not used to any movement, and now a transit of such length, such sweeping change, disoriented and racked their newly moving bodies.

In China, the families were separated into smaller cohorts to get on another set of large planes that would take them to their final destinations of resettlement — Australia, America, Europe. The American cohort landed in Chicago, where the families, bonded by war, by camp life, and now by a journey to the unknown, compared boarding passes. They were different from one another.

Their cohort dwindled again — their built-up tribe fractured. The force of their sea, their large body of water, atomized into tiny droplets all over the globe.

And like the departure on the bus, Ree Ree realized that she would also never see these people again. An entire sea of people reduced to a lake then to a stream then to a trickle and then nothing to drink from her previous life but the drops of memory in her own small family.

Ree Ree's family were the only ones to get on their small plane heading to South Carolina, where they would live for a short while. The rest of the families went their separate ways to board flights that took them elsewhere.

When they landed, Ree Ree's nuclear family members held on to one another's hands. It was just them. Ree Ree remembers the noise at the airport — there was none. It was her, her family, and dead silence. Looking around for the refugee resettlement agency representative as if underwater, Ree Ree could not register a thing or hear a thing in this small airport in the middle of nowhere.

Marwa was despondent about leaving.

She thought the "Muslim Ban" of 2017 would make the decision for her, keep her in Iraq, but as an SIV case, she, Ali, and their three sons were able to make it through and be approved for resettlement in the US. They received notification of their departure in March 2017 with an unusually long ten-day notice. But would it be long enough, she wondered, to sell their belongings, dissolve their business, get what they needed for their three sons? Her family came to say goodbye piecemeal. On the day they received the notification of their departure, she took out all of her children's clothes — a storehouse of memories — and cried bitterly.

And then she gave all of their clothes away.

Her mother noticed that she was about to give away her marriage blanket and took it from her for safekeeping. She then told Marwa's son Ahmed, whose hands look just like hers — the delicate shape of the fingers, the thin, soft veining — "Look at your hand so that you may remember me. You will see me. You will feel me. You will feel my hand on yours."

At the airport in Turkey, Marwa had no idea who to talk to and what to do next. Someone was supposed to find them and assist them onto their next flight, but no one came.

Paralyzed, Marwa wondered, *What next?* They had left nothing material behind — they had sold their car, given up their apartment, handed over their business, gotten rid of all of their furniture. Other refugees don't always do that. They leave some things behind. A small piece of land for their sons who will one day ask them: "What have you left for me so I can stand? So I can use my life." They may pay rent for six months. Hedge their bets.

Marwa and Ali hedged no bets, left no cushion. They jumped in the dark with both feet and nothing to go back to. *Is this hell, purgatory?* she wondered. *Are we stuck in limbo?*

And for the first time in her life, Marwa felt like an abandoned child. Until this moment, she and her husband had been used to elderly wisdom, collective decision making — Ali's parents or her parents would be consulted. "What car should we buy?" "What house should we rent?" "Should we move to this district?" "Who should I marry?" "When should I plan to have children?"

"What do we do next, *yaba, yamma*?" But there was no *yaba* or *yamma* here. She held Ahmed's hand, hoping to feel her mother's.

And like a child asked to grow up too fast, Marwa made the

decision to move forward, to find the person who would take them on the next flight to Washington, DC, for their layover.

In DC, it was so cold. They arrived at night and stayed at a hotel. They understood later that the hotel stay, their ride to the hotel, and their meals were all expenses deducted from their "welcome" funds — the onetime stipend all refugees receive.[2] In DC, everything was confusing — the weather, the food, the time difference. She woke Ali up in the middle of the night frantic, scared that they had missed their flight.

When they first exited the DC airport, they saw a huge American flag. Her son Yousef, then three, loved an Iraqi song called "We Are All Iraq," which played constantly on Iraqi television. In the video to the song, many Iraqi flags waved, and Yousef would delight in their regal posture, their freedom in the wind. When Yousef saw the American flag, he quickly yelled out: "WE ARE ALL IRAQ." His three-year-old mind did not distinguish between the two flags. To him, they were the same. One national symbol indistinguishable from another, one place indistinguishable from another.

She laughed at his confusion, but underneath she thought, *This is it. Already. We have barely landed and my child believes this is his country. This is his flag.* At the campus apartments in Greensboro her children, while playing outside, would stand to salute the flag whenever the anthem played in the soccer field right next door. At first, it upset her to see the flag everywhere — a trigger, a reminder of days during the war.

"But I can separate between a government and its people," Marwa said softly.

"The people here are nice; they have helped us."

In Greensboro, we meet the refugee families we host when they first arrive at the airport.

In March 2016, I went with a group of Guilford College faculty, staff, and student volunteers to welcome the first family to be hosted by Every Campus A Refuge. We had already welcomed Cheps that January, but this was the moment we had been preparing for since the program's inception. It had been founded expressly to support families, especially the more recently displaced Syrians. We didn't know much about this family. We knew that they were Syrian — a woman, a man, and a young teenage boy. And we knew their names and their ages. I had been surprised by the age of the mother and father — well into their late fifties, early sixties — and the age of the boy, a young teenager still, no more than fourteen. I thought perhaps they were his grandparents, that something had happened to his mother and father. Perhaps they had died, killed in the conflict like the thousands of Syrians who had been killed by then and the thousands more yet to be killed.[3]

Our airport welcome group counted among them several Arabic speakers, including an older Palestinian woman who had been a refugee herself. As will always be our custom on such welcomes, we carried signs and anticipation. I saw her quickly, the Syrian mother. She was in a wheelchair, pushed forward by one of the airport grounds staff. This explained why the family needed a house with a bedroom and a bathroom on the first floor. I would come to learn that the woman had significant rheumatoid arthritis. While she was able to walk, doing so was always painful and labored, especially up and down stairs. Thankfully, the house in which they stayed on our campus had no stairs.

The vestibule in Greensboro's small regional airport that leads from the gates and is prohibited to non-ticketed passengers is long and visible — the waiting and the waited-for can see each other through a glass partition and across black rope dividers for many long minutes, long enough for Um Fihmi and Abu Fihmi to understand that we were there for them.

Being able to see us as they made their way down the long corridor had been so unexpected that Um Fihmi, who was the woman in the wheelchair, began to cry.

Many refugees, most of them in fact, do not really have any idea what resettling in the US will be like. They are provided rudimentary orientation classes in the country of departure[4] about basic cultural and legal expectations: Wear your seat belt, don't strike your children, here's how to wire money. Cheps, for example, notes that one of the most important things people should be told at orientation, but aren't, is that laws in the US are effective *immediately*. This may seem ironic to many of us who feel that the wheels of justice turn slowly here, but everything is relative, and to Cheps it feels like refugees do not get enough of an education on what could and would happen to noncitizens if they break the law.[5] He also feels they should get a better education regarding how long it takes and how difficult it is to become a citizen — the many qualifications and requirements, especially of having lived a "good, clean life."[6]

Blaise, with only two days to get everything done before his departure, had to receive all the necessary vaccinations in one day. It exhausted him so much and made him so sick that he does not remember a single thing from the orientation class he attended two days before he got on a plane at an airport that bloomed into a church. Marwa received no orientation. She had to ask other Iraqis who left before her family about what to bring here and what to expect.

Later, in a conversation with Um Fihmi, she told me that seeing us at the airport was one of her happiest moments. She had no idea what was waiting for her on the other side of that long journey from Amman. She had fully expected to arrive and be escorted to live in a trailer. Being (quite literally) welcomed to the US was such a surprise, and such a relief. But then came another kind of cry: As I stepped away from embracing Um Fihmi at the airport, the older Palestinian woman in our group embraced her too and said to her in Arabic — "Do you see how we have been exiled?" — using the passive of *migrate* to indicate a fate wrought upon them, not of their own will. A more accurate translation would be "Do you see how we have been migrated?" In other words, we have not chosen this fate.

As we were busy with joy and welcome, completely engrossed in a moment of false hope that resettlement somehow means the end of a painful journey and the beginning of a happier, better one, these two women recognized that they were continuing to exist in the margins in some other country, away from home.

Indeed, while resettlement is a fate better than many refugees will ever realize — life in the camps so often mired in generational poverty, statelessness, and lack of opportunity — it is still filled with hardship. I have learned that it does refugees a great disservice to assume that resettlement means happiness[7] or is the solution to their trauma and pain. Such a view can blind us from seeing the ways in which resettlement is incredibly difficult, and it can elide refugees' sadness and pain — their homesickness, lack of sense of belonging, and depression — framing them as ungrateful rather than simply human.

The first few days are often the hardest as newcomers adjust not only to the new (ab)normal but also to the exhausting expectations thrust upon them. Refugees arrive after having spent hours and hours — sometimes days — of travel across airports and terminals. They have been interminably awake. And upon arrival, there is the strangeness of strangers, the drive in a place unknown to an apartment unknown with people unknown.

When Blaise arrived, he says, he was so tired that he felt nothing. He just wanted to sleep.

But he couldn't sleep. Was not allowed to go to sleep. He needed to stand there and listen to instructions on how to use this appliance and what this lease means and what that button does.

At the airport in DC, after a grueling trip of emotional and physical exhaustion, Ali and Marwa were asked to sign the

contract for repaying their plane tickets — something all refugees must do on the idea that this first loan will help them establish credit history in this country, which is useful for future large
purchases.

For some families this could be a $10,000 loan or more. That was
the case for an eleven-member DRC family we hosted.

Ali was afraid to sign; again, that abandoned-child feeling.

"Where are you, *yamma*? Where are you, *yaba*?"

They were not there, and so he signed.

I know this fear Ali is describing to me — the fear of an unimaginable unknown, unimaginable because even its basic contours
cannot be seen. I have seen this dread on the faces of all of the
guests we hosted.

I saw it on Abu Fihmi's face when, after he studied for the driving exam, we went with him to the DMV. He looked at the exam
screen as if looking into darkness — his face blood-drained, his
eyes glazed over. He did not pass the exam.

I saw it on Um Fihmi's face when I told her that her son Tamer's
school report had come in and that he was failing because he
missed too many classes. "What days," she asked, breathlessly. I
told her. She looked at me, into the darkness, face blood-drained,
eyes glazed. "Those are the days he had to come with me to the
doctor's appointments to interpret for me."

I saw it on her son Noor's face — he joined his mother later —
when I told him that the doctors couldn't diagnose his debilitating
condition. There didn't appear to be anything physically wrong
with him — nothing to explain the lethargy, the dizziness, the
inability to get up and go to work. Nothing but the trauma of the
war, I thought.[8]

I saw it on Cheps's face when we went to the facilities office at
Guilford College so he could sign his lease for the campus house.
The lease, even though the house and its utilities were free, allowed

Cheps to have an address, very important as the government would need to have one on file to send him necessary paperwork. But he held the paper in his hand, his eyes unseeing, and refused to sign that day.

I saw it again on Cheps's face when I went with him to the college cafeteria — an excellent one by many standards — for the first time.[9] Amid the myriad food stations — the salad, the vegan, the omelets and pizzas, the hot bar — Cheps found nothing to satiate his hunger.

Every time we went, he would fill his plate with sauceless pasta. Nothing else tasted like home.

One of the more damaging myths about refugees is that all they need is their "community," a problematic assumption that presumes people from the same place are indeed all the same and that they will get along. We know that this is not true in Cheps's case: Being a gay man made him vulnerable within the Ugandan immigrant and refugee communities and elsewhere. In fact, anyone who has fled dirty wars, civil wars, or sectarian/ethnic wars is likely to be at odds with, if not in danger from, others who were displaced by the same conflicts.

The arrival of Ree Ree's family, like those of many other refugees, had been terrifying. They had not been told that there would not be someone waiting for them as they exited the plane, that they needed to walk to the entrance of the terminal. Currently an active Every Campus A Refuge volunteer, Ree Ree notes this fact every time we are waiting at the airport to catch sight of new arrivals we have gone there to meet, often seeing them long after the plane had landed.

"They don't know they need to exit the airport," she always says. "No one told them." Thinking that someone will come get them at the gate, they wait with their IOM bags around their necks, hoping someone will recognize the symbol and claim them.

Ree Ree's family was finally claimed by their refugee resettlement agency case manager, a white woman. She was accompanied by a white pastor and an Asian woman with a child who was Burmese and would serve as their interpreter.

In the car, they introduced themselves. "What language do you speak?" they were asked. "Karen or Burmese?" "Karen," they said, though they speak both. This will matter later.

At the welcome house, there was food for them and sodas. Ree Ree was astonished.

"Can we eat this?" Ree Ree asked, eyeing the chicken and Pepsi. It was the most food Ree Ree had ever seen. She immediately monetized it, laborized it. Thought about how long, how many hours of work, how many dragged bamboos and broken backs it would take to buy that much food.

Their new life in America was nice in the very beginning, but it got hard quickly. The unaffordable rent, her dad's mistreatment at Chick-fil-A, the racism they encountered in a largely segregated southern town.

And worst of all, their interpreter was abusive. Though she was Burmese, like them, she had come to the US on a visa and believed that the refugees who came from the camps were "backward, uneducated." Not knowing that they also spoke Burmese, she would humiliate them to others as she talked on the phone about them, right in front of them. The abuse escalated — she would use their food stamps when she helped them with grocery shopping, would leave her child with Ree Ree's mother for free childcare without also leaving diapers or food, and would take the nicest clothes and toys from the agency before giving the remaining, less desirable items to their family.

"Why did she have so much power?" I asked Ree Ree.

"Because we didn't know what was going on. We thought this was normal."

The agency simply assumed that Ree Ree's family and the interpreter would bond — that because they were from the same country they would automatically love each other, look after each other. They failed to account for human differences and idiosyncrasies, for the simple human fact that people from Burma, just like Americans, come in all shapes, and sizes, and with a variety of intentions in their hearts.

Beyond the challenges of first arrival, refugees experience significant barriers to successful integration, to thriving rather than simply surviving. Without question, the challenges refugees face in affording safe housing, accessing appropriate health care, and finding fulfilling and well-paying work[10] are not unique to refugees. Many native-born Americans and immigrants face similar challenges. However, refugees also experience the added barrier of language — which affects how they navigate even the most basic of services and systems — and the trauma they carry. After all, refugees are here because they were running from death, having stared down the barrel of a gun, endured the fists of a mob, survived a bomb in a fridge or a cannon blast to the wall of their home, or evaded a sleeping hippo in the pursuit of a safe haven.

When refugees resettle in the US, they receive the small onetime stipend — as part of America's reception and placement program — to secure housing, furnishings, food, and so on. The period for them to receive support and case management is set at three months. After that, refugees are expected to achieve self-sufficiency.

Such little time is given to refugees to settle in, to breathe, to adjust. They find themselves almost immediately chased by the specter of poverty and debt (including one incurred before arrival — the airfare that needs to be paid back). These financial exigencies mean that the first and foremost necessity for refugees is to secure employment. Indeed, refugees are expected to accept the first job they are offered, and which is almost always non-commensurate with their

skills, certifications, degrees, or interests, an added barrier being that
many certifications and degrees from their home countries are not
recognized in the US. The first available job opportunity is usually
manual labor in a factory: food and meat processing or packaging.

And this expectation to find employment immediately inevitably overtakes other needs necessary for successful integration
— learning English and taking the time to adjust emotionally,
mentally, and culturally.

When Ali arrived in the US, like so many refugees before him he
had to take the first opportunity for employment presented to
him in order to provide for his family of five — his wife and three
young boys ages three to eleven.

As a child, Ali had grown up loving to draw — especially nature:
A palm tree next to a modest hut was a recurring motif. He was
left-handed — a difficult (*a'sar*) condition in the Arab and Muslim
world. His mother tried to make him right-handed. But he would
drop the food from his right hand, insisting on using his difficult
left hand. And it was his left hand that brought him the joy of
calligraphy. His talent as an artist was nurtured by the rich support
systems available for all children in Iraq at the time, especially
after-school and summer programs. These free centers provided
transportation, meals, activities, and education focused on sports,
culture, arts, performing arts, and sciences. His teachers would
motivate him with the gift of art supplies.

This passion for art was encouraged by his father, who worked
for a state newspaper and owned a private typesetting and design
business. As the paper's head designer, his father created the layout
and selected the fonts, working during the night to set the type for
the next day's issue. Often Ali would go with his father to work and
enjoyed being there — running errands, riding the elevator up and
down, watching the printing machines. During the day, his father
would take Ali to his private business office, where Ali would

deliver his father's designs to clients for tips. One summer, when he was in fourth grade, he made 60 Iraqi dinars, back when the Iraqi currency was strong and the dinar was worth $3. He bought with that money a small golden Qur'an and a chain to hang it on. It fell and his sister, not seeing it, swept it up in the sewer cleaning the house one day.

Ali fell in love with printing and design; doing well in them brought him joy and pride. This love continued to grow in middle and high school. His father taught him to work with the quill, and he pursued art in vocational school and then at university, learning to design everything by hand. When Ali graduated, he first worked with his father in his private business and eventually opened his own. After retirement, his father — whose own craft was done by hand in an increasingly technological world — would visit Ali in his office, giving him advice on his designs: Change this color, make this shape smaller, change this font.

The *aya* now reversed — the father visiting the son.

Even though Ali enjoyed significant national and international recognition — his art was exhibited at national galleries in Iraq and Jordan, and he was chosen to design and write the first page of a national publication of the Qur'an — his most prized possession is a simple painting he drew when he was eighteen years old in 1987, made up of basic geometric and floral designs. His wife jokes that the painting is only one year older than her, and that Ali is old, so very old.

Ali is proud — proud of that simple painting, of being so appreciated in Jordan that he received the difficult-to-achieve work permit and residency there, of being selected to design God's word: *It is We who have sent down the Remembrance, and We who watch over it.*[11]

When Ali came to the US, he thought, imagined, that he might be able to work in something related to his skill set, his passion, his education. He has since learned that almost all refugees end up working in jobs completely unrelated to their chosen fields due to the challenges of recertification. "If you loved doing something, you needed to forget it," he says. The refugee resettlement agency asked him what he would like to do, but none of that mattered — neither their questions nor his answers.

For the first few months, he worked at a local Japanese restaurant where the pay was too low to afford rent once they had moved off campus; but soon, positions opened up at the Tyson processing plant[12] located more than an hour away in Wilkesboro. The pay was decent — not great, but not minimum wage either — and the overtime opportunities were enticing. The Tyson factory in Wilkesboro employs many refugees from Greensboro who carpool together in minivans and cars. Ali owned a car, and he made additional money by picking up four other refugee employees from all over Greensboro and dropping them off at home on the way back. This meant that every day he would have to get up at 5:00 A.M., shower, make his dawn prayer, take his diabetes medication, and be at work at 8:12, when he had to punch in his card. He then had to be at his spot on the cutting line within three to four minutes decked in his gear, gloves, glasses, and earmuffs. At the end of the working day, he would leave at 5:00 P.M. and be home around 8:00 — the long commute back, the various stops to drop off his car mates.

The commute is a world unto itself, a microcosm headed to the macrocosm. In the car with him were refugees from Eritrea, Sudan, Burma, Egypt. They spoke English with one another and French, Swahili, Karen into their phones. After the bustle of the first ten minutes, things would quiet down, magically, sacredly, as everybody fell asleep to the car's gentle hum and sway. Everyone but the driver — left to listen to his favorite music. It would be the same on the way back. The first ten minutes bustling with the eating of snacks, bits of gossip, the complaints

— people smelled like fried food and incense — and then things would quiet down again, sacredly, mag⸱⸱ally, and everybody would sleep all the way home but the driver. The 2019 COVID pandemic, of course, put an end to those small worlds, those small joys, when bodies together in community would come to mean danger and death.

The work at Tyson was exhausting and painful. During the early days of his employment there, Ali blamed himself for ending up in that situation. He played his decisions like a reel of film in his head and wondered if a life like this was better than a dignified death in his home country — a fridge bomb catching him suddenly, painlessly, his hand drawing out the lovely letters of a wedding invitation or the sweeping loops of a greeting card. At Tyson, this same hand hurt so much from the constant motion of the up-and-down, up-and-down cutting. At night, he would sob from the depth of his pain; illuminated by the glow of the fridge, he put his hand in the freezer to numb it — a ticking time bomb. All he can do now is wear a wrap, take his medication, and get used to the motion — the up-and-down, up-and-down of the cutting.

And he has been used to it now for four years. He is a "shoulder cutter," a class 7, the highest difficulty of cutting, fit for his difficult left hand. The worker next to him cuts the wing, and the one next to him the breast. By the time the chicken reaches the end of the line, it is just bones. Ali has to cut thirty-six shoulders a minute. He moves his left hand — the one classified as difficult, the one he uses to do the most difficult work the processing plant has to offer — up and down, up and down at least thirty-six times a minute. But in truth, both hands hurt. One cuts, the other pulls. Thirty-six times a minute. To give their workers some kind of reprieve from the waiting time bomb of frayed nerves, Tyson switches their cutters' classifications every two hours to change the range of motion for their hands. He moves from class 7 to class 5, from cutting shoulders to cutting breasts. All the workers switch, like bees bustling to their new stations and back. But it doesn't help. Not really. It's the same hands, the same knife, the same chickens.

And the work is dangerous in other ways too. Once, the cutter next to him accidentally struck him with the knife when he lost control of his up-and-down and his range of motion went a little too far. He sliced Ali's arm. Others have cut their fingers, gotten their heads cracked when chicken cases fell on them. Ali is quick to say that Tyson tries to protect them as much as possible, both proactively and reactively.

Ali is loyal to Tyson. He wants to take pride in his work, and being valued by his company is one of the ways in which he can feel joy in what he does. He remarks on the extra pay, vacations, incentives, insurance. But he knows this is because the work is hard and far away, and without all of these perks, Tyson cannot get or retain workers.

Ali is a diabetic, and his monthly insulin and medication were a source of significant financial anxiety. The constant standing, the constant cutting motion, the bringing down of the hand in endless repetitiveness as he slices through frozen chicken carcasses, has permanently affected Ali's left arm, his writing arm. It is now riddled with frequent excruciating pain and spasms. This is what an artist capable of producing incredible, highly salable work as well as teaching art and calligraphy has to do to survive and support his family.

Many refugees can tell similar stories — about talents squandered and passions unmet.

Another significant challenge refugees face is securing safe and affordable housing.[13] This has only gotten worse over the years.

Refugee resettlement agencies used to be able to form successful relationships with landlords who would agree to lease to yet-to-arrive refugees, secure in the knowledge that their new tenants would get Social Security numbers and find employment shortly after their arrival. Increasingly, landlords are loath to rent to anyone who is not already here, who cannot show a track record of steady employment through paystubs and a clean credit history. These are things impossible for refugees to achieve while still en route, and they need places to stay as soon as they arrive. If they are lodged in hotels until their housing situation can be established, the funds to pay for the hotel come out of their limited onetime welcome stipend and will be exhausted quickly.

The difficulty in finding housing is sometimes aggravated by the make-up of refugee families. Often multigenerational (with elderly parents and several children), refugees are rarely able to find affordable multi-bedroom (more than two or three) housing. Housing laws specify how much square footage is reasonable for a human body to inhabit[14] — a certain way of understanding architecture and its functions, a certain way that does not account for lovingly shared beds and rooms and walls and meals, of doors always open for all the aunts, uncles, and cousins.

Affordable (let alone safe) housing is nigh impossible to find and completely out of reach for refugees who have been forcibly displaced with nothing but what they could carry with them and have just left refugee camps with little to no financial resources.

This dire situation has, like everything else, created a situation ripe for abuse and exploitation. Slumlords, knowing the urgency with which refugees need housing as well as their newness to the complicated landscape of American housing systems — especially tenant rights and renter responsibilities — and thinking that refugees are friendless, rootless, with no one to worry about or advocate for them should something happen, take advantage.

Yes, refugees experience significant barriers to successful integration — a condition in which, having escaped death, they ought to have an opportunity to thrive rather than simply survive.

And sometimes, they do not survive at all.

In May 2018, I was parked outside a grocery store when a flurry of messages came in on my WhatsApp, the preferred method of communication between internationals, even when they are in the same country. They were from Jennifer, the teenage daughter in a family from the Democratic Republic of the Congo (DRC) we had hosted on our campus from September 2017 to April 2018. They were now living in an apartment complex in Greensboro that had a large DRC refugee tenant population. They came to Greensboro because the eldest son in the family, when his case was separated from theirs when he turned eighteen, had resettled here before them. And so they joined him first in Greensboro and later in the apartments on Summit and Cone.

Jennifer was deeply affectionate. She would frequently text me pictures of herself in her colorful Sunday best, the new clothes she bought, the yellow purse she loved. So when the flurry of messages came through, I thought they were of the same sort — a teenage girl's excitement about beautiful things to wear, to hold.

They were not.

Instead they were images of small children. One image for each child — five altogether, two of them in hospital beds with tubes attached to their arms and oxygen masks on their faces.

I was unsure of what I was looking at, and about to write back, when she sent me another image of five children, laughing, standing outside the apartments at Summit and Cone in the central quad. The image had been edited with X's superimposed on three of the children. "Pray for the other two," the next message said. I recognized the kids. Just a month back, they helped us unpack when we went over to the apartments to move Jennifer and her family into the complex. Eager and excited, they took the small items we gave them from the trucks — the throw pillows, the toaster, the broom — and ran with them into Jennifer's new house, right next to theirs.

On May 12, 2018, in the early hours of the morning, Jennifer and the rest of the entire apartment complex, all forty-two units of it, were woken by the sounds of the children's father screaming for them as he burned inside their apartment.[15]

The mother was working third shift. She would arrive soon to see her children's bodies laid outside, on the pavement. She would get off the bus exhausted and think that, just like any other day, any other 4:00 A.M. arrival, she would come home and crawl into bed. She would see the children in the morning, make them breakfast, and send them off to school.

But the night sky was unusually colored this time — red, and amber, and blue flashes and swirls and haze — the color of the fire mixing in with the colors of the ambulances, the fire trucks, and the police cars.

And her children were not tucked into their beds. They were on the pavement. Why were they on the pavement? It was so cold on the pavement. So cold. Why were they so cold?

The family, just like other families in the complex, had complained often about the malfunctioning electric gas stoves. Their lights would come on, indicating that the ovens were lit even though nobody was cooking anything. That night, the father woke up to a closeness in his chest, a cough in his throat, and heat on his flesh. He jumped out of the second-story window and then realized he needed to go back in and get his children. Three of them died that night. Two later in the hospital. Roy Hope (eight), Lisa Josiane (seven), Christopher Danny (five), Joshua John (five), and Trump Emmanuel (two) — named after the president of the country that had welcomed them, that they thought would keep them safe.

The fire investigation found hundreds* of code violations, and the City of Greensboro condemned the complex. The hundreds of refugee residents, all having escaped wars in Uganda and the DRC, had thirty days to leave their homes — yet again.

Another timed departure from hell.

We helped Jennifer's family relocate to another apartment, hoping that this time the heaven of refuge would live up to their dreams of it and let them live.

When the COVID-19 pandemic arrived in the spring of 2020, it hit the refugee communities especially hard.[16] Living in tight quarters and traveling and working with others in such close proximity with no chance of self-isolation, newcomers contracted the disease quickly and in high numbers. When Blaise fell ill during the very early days of the pandemic, the very real fear of the effects of the virus brutalizing the refugees we were supporting, and who had already endured a trauma most people would find hard to imagine, pierced us.

"I am home alone, and I am very scared," Blaise told us.

In those early days, there were bodies of COVID victims left in homes and no one allowed to enter to collect them. Would his be one of them? The world saw people beseeching — "Please, come take my loved one away. I have had all I can take of watching over their pale body, unasleep, in their bedroom."

When Marwa left Iraq with Ali and their children, her parents didn't blame her. But then her mother got very sick after her depar-

---

* "Code Violations Found After 5 NC Children Die in Apartment Fire," CBS 17 (Raleigh, NC), May 27, 2018, https://www.cbs17.com/news/code-violations-found-after-5-nc-children -die-in-apartment-fire/; and Adaure Achumba, "After Deadly Fire, City Officials Find Many Code Violations at Summit Avenue Apartment," WFMY NEWS 2 (Greensboro, NC), May 24, 2018, https://www.wfmynews2.com/article/news/local/after-deadly-fire-city-officials -find-many-code-violations-at-summit-avenue-apartment/83-558014737.

ture and said to her: "There is a burning, a fire in my heart since you left. May Allah never burn your heart over a child." When Marwa's youngest child, Yousef, was admitted to the hospital, she kept thinking about this parting phrase. Up until that point, she had not told her family back home that her household was infected with COVID, but when it looked bleak for Yousef, she couldn't stop herself from calling

"What is wrong, my child?" her father asked breathlessly. No good calls come at night. "My heart has been pricking me for two days."

"I just want to ask my mother about that word."

"What word?"

"I want to know if my heart is about to burn?"

Marwa was about to give birth to her fourth son when Ali, who caught the virus at Tyson, brought the sickness home.

She had been so careful, minimizing her trips to the doctors' offices during her last trimester, when the pandemic arrived here in full force in the US, so that she wouldn't catch anything at the clinics. Initially, they thought they had escaped the plague. Tyson tested the workers, and those who had it were informed quickly and discharged. Ali was informed a full ten days after his test, while she was at the hospital giving birth to Adam. He called her while she was in her hospital bed to tell her. Her heart dropped.

Ali stayed home from work for two weeks, but Marwa wanted him out of the house. In the small, cramped quarters, her fear, especially for her three young children and a newborn, consumed her. And so Ali got out of the house by working delivery. When at home, he sat alone in a corner with a mask on. All the windows open. She, sitting upstairs.

For refugee families resettling in the US, isolation is a cruel joke — where and how do you separate families with nowhere else to go? Families who share walls, and meals, and rooms?

Marwa didn't know she was infected when she started her labor in May and called me to take her to the hospital. I hadn't seen her since March — a shock to the body considering that we visited with them nearly every day before the pandemic-induced shutdown. She and I would drink tea, eat cake or cookies, and watch Arabic song performances on her TV that streamed hundreds of Arab satellite networks. I was partial to the channels from the Gulf that televised music salons — seated-on-the-ground greats singing their classic songs, accompanied by seated-on-the-ground musicians, backup singers, and clappers. Occasionally, a couple of men or women would be moved to dance, to rise and sway with the rhythm of the drums and the oud. The kids — her three and my two, all between the ages of six and twelve — would play inside the cramped apartment, using the short, carpeted staircase as a slide or making forts out of umbrellas or playing out front in the square concrete yard or just beyond on the grass and in the small twiggy woods with its own creek.

When I saw her again in May, I couldn't embrace her as we usually did. I stood far away as her eldest opened the back seat for her. Double-masked, I opened the car windows and drove the two miles to the hospital. We couldn't go to the usual place women in Greensboro gave birth — and where I delivered both of my girls — because they had converted that to the COVID hospital. Before the pandemic, Marwa had done the customary tour of the women's hospital so she could see what was in store for her. Instead I dropped her off at the place where one of my dearest colleagues would go to get his late-stage pancreatic cancer treated. When I opened the back door for her, the hospital staff member out front asked if she needed a wheelchair. I knew she was scared. How could she not be? Alone, without her mother and sister, who had been with her in Iraq when she gave birth to her first three boys, she was entrusting herself to a complete stranger, in a strange hospital, in a strange land.

At the door, the man told me that I would not be allowed in with her. She bore the news with a bravery customary to Marwa, and I was slightly relieved to be released of this responsibility.

In Iraq, Marwa always had someone with her — through the pregnancy and at the birth, someone to watch the other kids while she was at the hospital. This time, no one was with her or with the kids. Ali would visit her for ten minutes to bring her the things she needed, and together, they would worry about the three they left at home.

During the pregnancy, her sister asked her to record the sound of Adam's heartbeat when she went to the doctor's office to listen to it so she and her girls could hear it too. During one of her pregnancy wellness visits, Marwa had taken the boys with her. Her mother babysat them on WhatsApp, talking to them, asking them questions, watching over them.

One night during her pregnancy Marwa had bled, and with Ali at work she had to learn how to use Uber to go to the hospital. In the car, she cried bitterly — "Do I worry about myself or the three kids I left at home?"

Marwa felt alone. She wished she could reach out to someone across the vast distance, hold their hand and watch all her children playing, their specters reflected happily on the walls.

When Adam was born and Marwa was able to take him home, the household became busy with the new baby. She had wanted a girl desperately but loved this new boy with the same fierceness she had all the others and with the same desperation she had wanted a girl. Perhaps this was why when the entire family got the virus and it was mostly mild — she had chills and lost her sense of taste and smell, the older boys had headaches — it was easy to miss what happened with the six-year-old Yousef, her youngest child until Adam's birth.

Yousef seemed tired and lethargic, but with a new baby in the house and his own position as the littlest suddenly gone, no school to go to, no friends to take his mind off the strange newcomer at home, it was easy to see his lethargy as an emotional response. But then he didn't get better.

"May your heart never burn like mine."
What did you mean, yamma?
Did you know something was going to happen?
Do you blame me for leaving you?
Have you forgiven me for leaving you?
I know that our bodies are intertwined — that whenever I was pregnant, you would be the one to get sick; that when I went into labor, your body would be racked with pain; and now that Yousef is lying in the hospital, you are burning, and it is my duty, even though I am burning, to put out your flames. To hide my pain. To hide the fear.

They took Yousef to the hospital. He was tested for COVID, but it was incorrectly "not detected." He went back home. But he still didn't get better. His eyes turned red. On a telehealth appointment, Marwa described this new symptom to the doctor on the call. She told me how the doctor's face changed immediately.

"Bring him now."

Only one parent could go with Yousef to the hospital — the shut-down protocols were at their most severe. So Marwa, who does not drive and was caring for a month-old baby, waited at home while Ali took Yousef to the hospital. He was admitted to the children's ICU and then transferred to the hospital at Chapel Hill, an hour and a half away. His father, Ali, had to make the long drive in his own car following behind the ambulance that carried his little son's quickly failing body.

Marwa could only see her son on a screen — bloated and unresponsive. If she called Ali and he didn't answer, she would crumble with fear and burning.

"Swear you are telling the truth. Swear he is still alive."

Doctors and then interpreters explained his condition to her at length — she loved biology as a student, and her sister is a nurse in Iraq. I marveled at her ability to keep all the medical details straight, understanding their intricacies, asking me questions so I could ask the doctors in English. They decided to give him steroids, and he improved quickly.

Yousef is all better now. His body deflated to its normal size, his skin returned to its usual light-brown color, but he needs to go back and see the heart doctors for a potentially long-term side effect.

His mother's heart is permanently damaged.

Refugees are refugees because they want to save their children. To face their child's death through the lens of a phone camera is not something they bargain on in the land of exile. They bargain on their own misery, their own loneliness, their own homesickness — but not on their children's sickness in their new home.

It is harder yet for Ali, who feels an overwhelming guilt for being the reason for his son's illness. He brought it home, carried it in his loving breath and difficult hands classed for difficult work — a time bomb ticking in a fridge until it exploded on Yousef. Ali tries to forget the days he spent with Yousef in the intensive care unit like a criminal trapped with a new disease, unknowing doctors coming and going in their astronaut suits and only a chair to sleep in, listening in horror to the mysterious machine attached to his son's body, its changing sounds signaling impending death.

Those memories are immovable, harder to extract than the shrapnel in his back, the bullet hole in his leg.

Resettlement carries refugees like dust in the wind, like drops of water, to the far corners of the earth, thousands of miles away from their souls that used to be right next door.

Resettlement asks them to leave whole lives behind in the span of days. And hard though that life in an urban or warehouse camp may be — safer perhaps than the persecution that necessitated its existence — it is a life one gets accustomed to, a very long chapter (sometimes decades long) in one's not-set-down story.

Resettlement takes large built-up families, a sea of people, and reduces them to lakes, then streams, then trickles, then drops of water that splash on the windows of small planes headed for the small towns and cities of the "first world."

Resettlement makes them feel like abandoned children forced to grow up too fast, and alone. And suddenly, all alone, to figure out how to live — not just to visit, but to live — in an unknown place with an unknown people.

Resettlement expects them to get along with, to want to be around, others who look like them or who come from the same country or the same region, when, in fact, they might be the enemy.

Resettlement does not know that like all humans, they come in all shapes and sizes, and with unique and individual hearts and intentions.

Resettlement makes them use their hand, so precious it produced the most difficult calligraphy to render God's words, to cut thirty-six chicken shoulders a minute instead. Resettlement makes their hand throb with pain only a fridge can cool, a ticking time bomb.

Resettlement is five children dead from a malfunctioning gas stove, their bodies cold on the pavement, their landlord continuing to make money renting to refugees all over the city.

FROM CAMP TO CAMPUS

Resettlement may carry refugees like dust in the wind, like drops of water, to the far corners of the earth. And refugees may feel like abandoned children set down to live — with no trial period, no time for error — among strangers in a strange place. But they are as far from weakness, as far from blowable dust, from evaporable water, as anyone can possibly imagine.

In my frequent talks about the refugee experience, I often challenge audiences who know little about refugees other than their suffering and precarious existence to think about the strength, the resilience, the unblowable groundedness, the inevaporable full-bodiedness refugees must possess to have made it to any point in their long and arduous journey.

When the bombs exploded, the bullets flew, the bloody machetes glistened in the sun, they swallowed the paralyzing fear that gripped them, gathered themselves, their children, and whatever they could carry, and walked. They walked for hundreds, sometimes for thousands of miles. They walked for days, sometimes for months. They walked across multiple borders and countries. Along the way, they slept on the bare ground, ate whatever grew from the cracks of the earth, took whatever boat, whatever train, whatever truck would get their children to safety.

And then, when they got somewhere a little safer than the place they'd left behind, they swallowed the agonizing anxiety that held them, and they talked. They talked for days, for months, sometimes for years. Even though the talking was painful, often humiliating, they talked about why they needed to leave their souls behind, and it was always because they needed to save their bodies or the little bodies they carried with them, on their backs, across rebelled borders, barbed wires, and dangerous rivers.

And then they waited. They swallowed the debilitating oblivion that overtook their lives, and they waited for years, for decades, hoping that the talking somehow mattered. They waited in make-shift tents, in underground apartments with crumbling roofs, in made-up cities on the edge of life.

And then the few, the so very few, the less than 1 percent, flew. They flew for days across countries, and oceans, and continents. And when they landed, they swallowed the overwhelming exhaustion that just wanted them to close their eyes and sleep, sleep for days, and instead they lived, wide-eyed with strangers in strange places.

Resettling refugees are the ones who, despite all the possible odds against them, made it. And it wasn't just luck. It was sheer strength, resilience, unblowable groundedness, inevaporable full-bodiedness.

Communities receiving resettling refugees can make the rough landing after that long flight, after that long wait, after that long talk, after that long walk, after that brutal war — a little softer.[1]

Cheps knew nothing about Greensboro before he arrived. He had to google it when he got to Chicago. But it didn't really matter.

"All I needed was protection, and I was happy with anywhere I could be able to live as long as I got protection from the violence which I ran from in my own country," he says.

In the early days, he rode his bike everywhere — especially to work on those cold and bitter January and February days. He wondered about the trees surrounding his house on campus behind the counseling center, right by the lake.

They looked dead.

I said, "They will come back to life."

In the spring, he got a car and began "setting up his life." He found his way to the foods he loves at his favorite stores: G Mart and Compare Foods. Now he always makes poisho, a mixture of flour and water — the Ugandan fufu. And now he is thinking about a house.

In Uganda, the tradition is that the father will have to *start the life* of his child. At least, give them something to get them started — a small piece of land or a house. His own father had left him land in Uganda. It is on this land that he is building a house for his son now. And now he has another son here. And Cheps needs to set him up too.

But otherwise, Cheps is realistic. He understands that he will have to break from other parts of the tradition. When Cheps grows older, his son will not be able to take care of him because everyone has to work in the US. In Uganda, had he been able to stay, he would have run a small business that kept him going and allowed him to spend time at home and with family. Here he has to work. As eventually will his son. No one will be there to take care of Cheps when he grows older.

And so Cheps works — hard. He started off at $8 an hour, and now he makes nearly $19 as a forklift driver, nearly $20 if he picks up the second shift. Which he does frequently.

But this is a dangerous job. And it is very easy to kill someone if the driver is not very careful, watching for the people walking around, checking the mirrors on the ceilings, adhering diligently to the traffic lights.

He knows that there is no walking away from a forklift accident — if he hits someone, they will be gone. And no amount of apologizing, no amount of moving money from one pocket to another, no amount of "talking nice" will do. Nothing will bring them back.

But the boss man wants the workers to go faster, to work quicker, to get the job done in less time. And the cameras are everywhere, watching how he is driving. He must be very careful of this new boat with a new beast — there is only so much his forklift can pick up without turning over, only so fast he can go without getting careless. And so Cheps knows he has to say no when he is indeed asked to go faster, to lift more. This is a boat he won't get on — where executing dangerous balancing maneuvers can tip everybody over into the deadly waters below.

Cheps loves being a forklift driver, but he would like to buy his own truck and drive state-to-state. He wants to start his own business in the future, a small one. To have time for family. And he thinks about the friends he left behind. Marcel, still planting, still watering, still waiting for someone "from the community" to be the face of his next interviewer for his set-down story.

"Do you know Matthew Shepard?" Cheps asks me.

Of course I do.

"That is what is happening to my community in Uganda — the bigger community will beat you up, hang you, throw you in the dumpster, treat you like trash."

It happens here, too, I thought. *Matthew Shepard happened here.*

We are all doing our best to survive boats with lions and to get to the other side.

The life Blaise built in Burundi is not destroyed. His new set-down story is an extension of the previous one. It uses the same words; the languages he caught from his parents have allowed him to now work here as an interpreter.

"Resettlement is like a jump in the dark from the edge of a precipice," he tells me. "You don't know what is on the other side — can only know when you get there, if you get there — how long of a jump it really is."

And the jump was shorter than he expected. When he got here, he was not alone. At the Every Campus A Refuge house, he stayed with two other young men also hosted by the program — Amani and Nasraldin.

Amani was from Rwanda, and they could speak together in

Kinyarwanda. Nas was from Sudan and spoke only Arabic. They communicated through smiles.

They lived like brothers in that 1920s house next to the football field on Guilford's campus. When Blaise couldn't get his food stamps activated for the first two weeks, he used Amani's. And by the time they were activated, there was no longer a distinction between Blaise's food stamps, and Amani's, and Nasraldin's. Like brothers, they would take turns paying for the household groceries.

Although Blaise felt like a helpless child when he first arrived, he began to feel that perhaps he could actually make it here. That he had something like a family — in his roommates, in the volunteers who came every day, in the friends he made on campus.

In addition to the newness of himself to this place, Blaise also found that America itself was new, that it was unlike what he had imagined. He thought it would be "shiny" like the America he saw in songs and movies; when he streamed America online, its buildings always looked lux, its cities rich, its roads smooth, large, and promising. He makes sure I understand that he does not think America is bad. After all, he muses, if a culture of 350 million people can contain those multitudes — if all of those people *can live with* that culture — then it is not bad. It *cannot* be bad. For Blaise — who went back and forth between cultures that could not contain him — there is so much appeal to the goodness of something that can withstand such a congregation of bodies, such diversity of breaths, such a plurality of ideas.

He can see that in America. But it is hard to look at that house (as he gestures to a single-family home), knowing that only one family lives there — and continue to see that. In Burundi, a house like that would be occupied by three families. "We like to live together, to gather around the food and each other," he tells me as he reminisces of a life he lived long ago as the child of two Marias and forty other family members in one compound. He so wants to see the continental embrace of the 350 million reflected in his own daily life, wishes he could go outside and easily say to neighbors, to strangers, to passersby — "Hi, how are you?"

He wants to make friends, "but it is not safe here — to make so many friends," he says.

Even dreams are hard to follow here. In Burundi, he was in his third year of studying psychology at the Université des Grands Lacs. He stopped abruptly when he was accepted for resettlement. Again, he had to start over. He could not continue his education because he could not afford to do anything else with his time but make money so he can survive, pay his rent, buy the basics. Going back to university is certainly out of the question for him at the moment. He needs to set down his new story first, and in this new chapter, there is no time to figure out who he wants to be. His life here is not as dangerous as a gun barrel to his head, but the decisions it forces him to make might be no safer than crossing a river filled with hungry hippos and clamping crocodiles. Once, to be able to get back to his job, which was out of town, he chose to spend the night outside at a gas station because he knew his fare would not be enough to take him home and back.

This experience has made Blaise a community helper — a pastor in the invisible church of newly arrived refugees, helping them cross the river and get to their job interviews whenever they need a ride.

Blaise is certain that if refugee resettlement officials were set down in another country and given the same treatment refugees are given here, they would not make it.

But he made it. To him, resettlement is a state of the heart. After the initial terror, he decided to embrace his new home even though he misses everything about his old one.

"For Americans, it must be the same, right, Diya? No place like home?" he asks.

"Yes," I say. "Perhaps it is the same for everyone."

"No," he says. "There is nothing like the chance at a second home."

We got a second home here. We only have to set down our stories in it.

Marwa suffers from the disease of perpetual homesickness. Even during her honeymoon in Erbil, a few hours from her home in Baghdad, she missed her home so much it felt like exile. Visiting God's house, Mecca, for a few days also felt like exile. At the departure for the greatest exile of all, she wailed so loudly the neighbors heard her. Yousef, then three years old, cried with her even though he knew not why he was crying. Her mother told her at that time: "If you ever want to come back, I will pay for your tickets."

Marwa likes to think this is still true.

But it is not. Neither for her, nor for her family. For her, every year the possibility for return grows more remote. The shackles increase — the kids' schools, their lives here. And for her mother — she has grown accustomed to Marwa not being there anymore. In the early days, they would talk every day. Her father would call her. Her brother Bakr would speak with her boys. Now the conversations have dwindled to a drip.

Marwa begs them to include her in their decisions and conversations: "Even if I am far away, please do not treat me like I am invisible. Please do not make me feel like I do not exist. Please remember me when things come up, when you sit together — family-meeting-style — to discuss things. When there is news, good or bad, do not put it in your head not to tell me because my body is not there. My soul is with you."

But they do.

Far from the eye, far from the heart.

While Marwa's family lived in their campus house, she would go walking frequently, looking for signs of home in the trees, the houses, the fields. And finding none, she would cry. Strangers would greet her. They saw her tears so often, they became friends. She was hearing from other refugees how different her own experiences upon arrival were because she and her family were hosted on a campus. "If I had experienced what they had experienced, I would have gone back, no question," she says. For Marwa and her family, the speed of resettlement happened more slowly, at a more humane pace. For others it seemed to follow an urgent trajectory: the looking for jobs, the working immediately (in shifts so that either mother or father could be home to watch the kids), the medical operations upon arrival, the setting up of life, the understanding of the culture. So many of their friends, they found out later, were scammed by those who take advantage of refugees and their newness to this country.

And yes, there was something beautiful about the kids riding their bikes on campus for hours, exploring the woods, throwing rocks in the lake. Her sister would tell her: "Stop advertising the beauty of the place, the house; stop talking about the cabinets, the spices, the volunteers. The eye of envy will cut you down."

Marwa suffers from the disease of perpetual homesickness, but she has changed much since she has been here. Outside of her family's logic now, she doesn't really understand why the divorced woman Bakr wants to marry is considered "lesser" or "incomplete" by her parents and sister. Or that he is "complete" and "perfect" by comparison. She doesn't discipline her children the same way her sister does, and she cries out in admiration when she sees something beautiful, compliments someone on their lovely shirt, unafraid that they will misunderstand her compliment for envy and drown her in their suspicion.

"Maybe I am a *herjai, zahrat al-althaloot*," she muses. A delayed flower, the *herjai* does not come in early spring. It blooms later, alone. Like the *herjai*, she feels a different blossoming whenever she talks to someone back home. But that too makes her feel alone. As if she doesn't belong to the people she left behind, as if she is not like them anymore. I remind her that this is what exile is: One does not feel at home in the new country and one no longer feels at home returning to the old country. Her family has stayed the same. She has changed.

A flower alone in a field, late-blooming.

She reminds me that not all people in exile change in that way — for the better. Some get worse. They forget completely who they are and where they came from. They do not intentionally plant themselves in new soil mixed with the old. She tills the old soil every day, refreshing her memories of Iraq constantly, playing them like a reel before her mind's eye whenever she can: a perpetual slide deck of all the things she and Ali did while they lived there, all the clothes they bought for each child on every Eid, so that she can remember them like a family album of the people who matter the most now.

"When you make the decision for exile, it is because you choose your children over your parents."

Of the refugee guests we have hosted on our campus, Marwa and Ali are the first to buy their own home. Marwa is happy they moved; the apartment they lived in when they left campus reminds her of what happened with Yousef, of when she said goodbye to him at the door when he left for the hospital with his father. Yousef had turned to hug her, but she had refused his hug because she did not want him to see her cry. She had turned her back and then almost never saw him again.

In the new house, she is scared to be happy. If she laughs, she believes something bad might happen. She is afraid — always afraid — of happiness. When someone expresses it, she wants them to limit that feeling, to hedge their bets.

"As Iraqis, we are afraid of laughter," Marwa says. "Of losing people. Even our lullabies are sad. We don't want the spirits to sense our happiness in our children and steal them away."

At night, in Iraq, her father would make Yousef cry with his sad voice in the *tahweedeh*.

My child, you are my child. My child, you are my child. Your enemy is far and living in the desert.

His voice held the same sadness when he sang about his brother who died — who was supposed to be a prisoner but was shot dead the first day of battle. The one he dropped off at the army barracks and who never returned.

She is so grateful that Yousef returned.

Ali holds on to the women in his life, the book with his mother's songs, and his memories. Oddly enough, being in the US has allowed him to reconnect with one of the most important women in his life — his beloved aunt, who was raised with them like a sister, who showered with him, took him to visit her friends, slept next to him on the rooftops. Long ago, a serious rift had occurred between this aunt's husband and her brother, Ali's father. Ibtisam took her husband's side, breaking her brother's heart. She was like one of her brother's children, their own father having died when she was very young. Her brother, Ali's father, raised her, paid for her education, her wedding, her surgeries, and doctors, and physical therapy to restore the motion in her arm, which was paralyzed after childhood polio.

A year before his father's death, Ali's aunt reached out to mend what was broken. She was on her way to visit the Prophet's grave and wanted to do so clean-hearted, slate emptied. But her brother refused and died angry with her. Loyal to his father, Ali could not mend what was broken while he was still in Iraq. The rest of his family would have felt betrayed.

Now in the US, Ali realized he could reconcile with her without his family knowing. Timidly, at first, he reached out to her on social media. She wrote back quickly with words of love. They exchanged messages and pictures. And then one day, he called her. And now they talk all the time, their physical distance from other family members making their restored love possible. Like a secret affair — carried out long distance — hidable, undetectable.

At Tyson, Ali has found ways to be proud of what his difficult arm has allowed him to achieve: He has made it onto the "Superhero Board" for never missing a single day of work without excuse or advance notice. Indeed, he is one of the few to make it to four years with no points, no blemishes on his record. Recently, he won a cartoon coloring competition, his prize a $100 gift card and art supplies and stationery that he gave to his children.

Using the campus's art studio and supplies, Ali produced new artwork, which was exhibited in the galleries of Guilford College and Greensboro Project Space. People are commissioning art pieces from him — on canvas, on plates, on glass. It is not necessarily a sustaining and sustainable job, but it is something that keeps his hand doing something other than cutting up and down, thirty-six shoulders a minute.

Whenever we welcome a new family to be hosted on campus, Ree Ree loves setting out that first feast, the welcome meal. She remembers how much her first meal — hundreds of bamboos-worth and laid out in abundance — made the soundless fear of her first arrival seem less soundless: the crunch of the chicken, the fizz of the Pepsi as they sat around eating silently with strangers at a strange table in a strange land.

But it is not chicken and Pepsi anymore. She thinks carefully about where the family is coming from — what kinds of spices they would have used, what kinds of meats they would eat or not, what kinds of vegetables grow in their part of the world — and she tries to make something with her own hands that tastes like home.

Ree Ree's initial loneliness eased a little in those early days when a newly arrived Muslim refugee family shared a house with hers. She enjoyed teaching the children all the things she felt she knew — a veteran newcomer — about how to grocery shop, what to wear to school, how to defend yourself against the bullies. And she enjoyed learning new things from them, like why the hijab, even when seemingly cumbersome, even when it stood in the way of fun, is not something one can easily stop wearing. It means something more than clothing, especially when one is a stranger in a strange land and trying to hold on to one's windblown, about-to-evaporate body.

When one of her uncles who had also been living in Tham Hin joined her family some months later, it seemed to Ree Ree that a sense of family — which had been so lost to her — began to re-form itself, if distortedly, in her new home.

Camp life doesn't disappear in resettlement. Ree Ree carries with her the lessons her mother taught her — informed absolutely by the exigencies of camp life. Once, at camp, one of her mother's prized cabbages — which she had been growing carefully, tending to lovingly, and set to win the "biggest cabbage" competition at the camp — was stolen. Even though she knew she would never get her cabbage back, her mother stood her ground, confronted all of the attendees, gathered the whole camp, addressed the community leader, and refused to acknowledge the validity of the competition. That fierceness runs through Ree Ree. She now works with refugee farmers in North Carolina, providing them with access to land so they can farm and sell their produce — so they can do the work they love, eat the food they love, and earn fair wages. The sneaking out, illegally cutting bamboo, breathless under its weight, back-broken, wishing instead for one's own land to farm in the way of one's parents and grandparents, bristles in Ree Ree's long hair.

Now her farm[2] says, *Please come, in the open, in the daylight, plant what you will, sell what you will.*

Um Fihmi lives in Buffalo, New York, now. Like Jennifer's family who moved from North Carolina to Tennessee, Um Fihmi and her family left the state to which they first arrived. Called secondary resettlement, this happens because refugees often cannot find the opportunities they hoped for, needed, in the location of primary resettlement.

"Will our migration ever end?" Um Fihmi asks me.

Her son Noor, the only one of her older children who was able to join her from Jordan, works as an Uber driver at night. During the day, he sleeps, his depression getting the better of him. Because all of her other children were over the age of eighteen, their cases were processed separately, and her other two sons and four daughters are still stuck in Madaba, waiting on the refugee resettlement agency to call them, to tell them their time has come to also join their mother and father. In the meantime, they use dwindling food coupons to pay for rent and work odd jobs whenever they can. Their own children do not go to school and have forgotten how to write their own names.

Um Fihmi swears to me that she would not have left her children behind in Jordan had she not needed to leave for two important reasons: her youngest son Tamer's future and her own health. In Jordan, Tamer was missing out on an education, and she wanted something better for him. A life of choice and opportunity. And her own body was failing her; she needed surgeries and medications, none of which she could access living as a refugee in Madaba.

Now she has access to the medical support she needs, and Tamer has just started college. But even though she has only "seen comfort in the US," her soul is sick. The sight of police officers carrying weapons terrifies her, ties her tongue, paralyzes her body; all she can see in them are those men who broke into her house in Homs, masked, guns drawn, pulling away her son, threatening to kill the entire family as they had done their neighbors.

And then there is the guilt that eats away at her. When her son Noor forces her to go out, to gaze upon her Lord's face in the beautiful streets and the water, all she can do is look at the beauty and wonder about what right she has to be here, to be watching the ships roll majestically into the harbor when her oldest son Fihmi is too depressed[3] to leave his own home, even during Eid. He is too embarrassed to greet his nieces and nephews and not be able to put his hand in his pocket — in the customary way — and pull out the *eidiyehh*, the money that tells them that he is their uncle and that Eid is a time of joy and plenty. Instead he sits at home in Madaba, disappearing into the size of a twig. His wife, Hazar's mother, left him and their children; she could no longer handle their poverty, no longer watch her children starve. In Jordan, there are not enough jobs for Jordanians, let alone Syrians.

Um Fihmi and Noor send what they can to their family back in Madaba, but she and her husband are too old and too sick to work, and Noor makes just enough to survive and care for his own wife and three children. She is in her sixth year without them. In the home country, they all lived in the same building, each son and daughter on a different floor.

She is in Buffalo, watching the ships roll into the harbor, and her children are living their own death — a rented life of fainting bodies under falling roofs, thousands of miles away in an ancient city with an old mosaic map.

"I have put my eye in God's eye. For I have nothing in my hands. It is all out of my control."

In resettlement, windblown, about-to-evaporate bodies set down and plant themselves in new soil tilled with the old. They take root quickly because they have to, for there is no time for anything else but survival. Their limbs grow strong so that they can hold up the fruit they bore, entwining with other trees windblown from other parts of the world for support or watching ships roll into the harbor as they dream of the old groves they left behind.

And when there is time, they will tend to their own blossoms, late-blooming but all the more beautiful.

NAMES AND NUMBERS

What's in a name?

The terms *refugee, immigrant, migrant, asylum seeker*, and *undocumented* are used interchangeably with alarming ease and frequency. While they each represent a human body on the move, they refer to different causes and reasons for this movement as well as different political and legal statuses.[1] Conflating these terms results in ideological stances that have real and negative consequences.[2] For example, in my work with refugees it has been clear that many of the audiences I have spoken with (in a variety of settings: universities, faith communities, local groups, and so on) about the refugee crisis and refugee resettlement conflate *refugee* with *asylum seeker* or with *undocumented*. Because the latter two are cast by US policies and rhetoric as dangerous and undesirable, this ideological framework gets extended to refugees as well. It was also clear that some conflate these particular experiences of "forced displacement" (a handy catchall term to refer to individuals for whom leaving home was made under duress) with "illegal" activities. This again is fomented by political rhetoric and ideologies that cast certain forcibly displaced individuals seeking succor at our borders (both literal and figurative) as *bad*. These individuals, then, in an unsurprising metonymy, become "illegal" themselves. A dangerous linguistic sleight of hand occurs here that allows our collective psyche to think of other human bodies as first simply unworthy of crossing into our territories, then unworthy of existing at all, then worthy of extermination.

Of course, there is nothing illegal about seeking sanctuary. Linda Rabben, in her book *Sanctuary and Asylum*, shows how the act of seeking sanctuary and refuge has been protected across centuries. And while it has shifted and changed over time and space, the fundamental act of throwing your body against the mercy of another when the lion is at your back is still considered so sacred that "undocumented" individuals under threat of deportation sheltered in sanctuary in places of worship across the US under the full view and knowledge of ICE.[3] Among the Bedouins,[4] the act of seeking sanctuary is sacrosanct and must be upheld, even at the risk of destruction to the sanctuary-giver. Stranger or friend, indeed even the enemy, can invoke sanctuary with the Bedouins — no questions asked — for three days. Any harm that comes to the sanctuary-seeker would be the responsibility of the sanctuary-giving tribesman and would bring great shame and dishonor to the entire tribe. To invoke asylum, the seeker must claim themselves an "entrant" — the Arabic word means both a person seeking immediate, lifesaving help and a guest not of the place but seeking membership and protection.

This act — to seek protection from imminent danger — is not only an age-old basic human right. It is also written into national[5] and international[6] laws; Article 14 of the Universal Declaration of Human Rights asserts the right of everyone to seek and enjoy asylum. The borders of the once-tribes, small towns, and villages have now expanded to the modern states. And the never-ending process of forging modern states — struggling to control their borders, expand them and defend them — has created the asylum seekers these very same states now seek to turn away from their borders, their doors. Peter Gatrell, in *The Making of the Modern Refugee*, shows how the political shifts of the twentieth century, chief among them the creation of modern nation-states through war and exploitation, have produced the largest numbers of forcibly displaced individuals in recorded history. That is a disaster unto itself. It is usually then followed by the disaster of amnesia (forgetting who was on the land before) and the delusion about who can claim original ownership. We have experienced a similar amnesia here in the US: forgetting that we are nearly all guests living on the stolen lands of those we now, in an unsurprising act of delusion, recast as "illegal" in the non-historical fiction of the ebb and flow of human migration and human movement.[7] To add insult to injury, we now want to deny the fundamental act of sanctuary, of seeking asylum, to those displaced by our own geopolitical and economic exploits in parts of the world many of us have never visited, and sometimes never heard of.[8]

Even though many of us are guests and the descendants of guests, some of us are loath to welcome new ones, to make strangers — as we and our ancestors have been made — into neighbors.

Refugee — While frequently used interchangeably with *immigrant*, *undocumented*, and *asylum seeker*, the term *refugee*, as it is used in current political parlance, refers to a particular individual who has been acknowledged as a refugee by the office of the UNHCR. This person is designated as a refugee because they *cannot* go back to their country of origin for fear of losing their life, and therefore "requires international protection."[9] The UNHCR, the United Nations' refugee agency, was established in 1951 on the heels of the largest forced displacement crisis of the modern world — created by World War II — to deal with the astronomical numbers of those forced to leave their homes due to conflict and persecution.[10]

To be designated or internationally recognized as a refugee "with access to assistance from states, UNHCR, and relevant organizations"[11] and become eligible for legal resettlement in a third country (though only a fraction of the world's refugees achieve such resettlement), you must prove that you are not able to go back to your country of origin due to a well-founded fear of persecution "for reasons of race, religion, nationality, membership of a particular social group, or political opinion."

This legal definition is important because it translates to a "legal" status, especially when refugees are resettled. For example, the US, which has been resettling refugees for decades, acknowledges the refugee designation as a "legal" status that comes with specific benefits for the person upon arrival in the country — a Social Security number, employment authorization, temporary medical insurance, immediate permanent residency, pathway to citizenship, and — though onetime and quite limited — financial support. A significant infrastructure has been built around supporting refugees in the US through refugee resettlement agencies and other service providers.

Besides the legal definition of the term *refugee*, there is, of course, the social and cultural use of the term. Anyone who has been forced to flee their home because of conflict and persecution and seeks shelter and safety elsewhere can and should be considered a refugee, and certainly there were many refugees well before the UNHCR was created. Most refugees are never resettled and never return to their country — living out their lives, for generations, in warehouse[12] and urban refugee camps in economically and politically beleaguered neighboring or transit countries, without fully integrating into the local community. Quite often, they remain peripheralized — physically on national borders and culturally and socially within urban landscapes.

The most recent statistics show that there are 26.4* million refugees in the world today. Of them, 20.7 million are under the mandate of the UNHCR and 5.7 million are Palestinian refugees, like many in my family, who are under the mandate of the UNRWA. Created in 1949, UNRWA supports the "relief and human development of Palestinian refugees" and their descendants displaced by the Israeli occupation of 1948 and subsequent Israeli expansion and encroachment over historically Palestinian territory.

* As of November 15, 2021. For the latest statistics, see "Figures at a Glance," UNHCR, www.unhcr.org/en-us/figures-at-a-glance.html.

Both the UNHCR and UNRWA definitions of refugees suggest a kind of interminability. Once you are a refugee (made so by the fact of the impossibility of return), should that one condition of non-refoulement remain present, you are always, in a sense, a refugee.[13] Palestinian refugees fall within a category of more heightened everlastingness where even the descendants of Palestinian refugees bear that status, the mark of exile.[14]

Displaced — Someone who has been forced to leave their home for whatever reason. There are more than 82.4 million forcibly displaced individuals in the world today. This number never stops increasing.

Asylum seeker — Legally speaking, a refugee in the making. A refugee is recognized as such and can enjoy international protection and assistance because their plight has been documented, and they have been registered or acknowledged by the international community as a refugee. An asylum seeker is exercising their human right to seek safety and asylum. They must make their case — that their life hangs in the balance unless they are taken in.

Migrant — In the New York Declaration for Refugees and Migrants, a resolution adopted by the UN General Assembly in its seventy-first session on September 19, 2016,[15] important distinctions between refugees and migrants are made. Migrants may sometimes move "without incident." In other words, they choose to move rather than being forced to move. Choice and force, however, are not objective concepts. One does not choose poverty, one does not choose climate disasters that burn towns, one does not choose a burning love for literature or astrophysics that cannot be quenched within a country's borders, one does not choose to love a person who has left and now expects the beloved to follow, one does not choose the businesses and corporations that flatten the country's resources and leave its people empty-handed. What is crucial here is the ability to return. For even if you are forced to move for one of those reasons, what makes you a migrant and not a refugee is that the return to your country of origin does not carry with it the same danger, the same fear for life and freedom. If return, readmission, refoulement are possible, then the individual is a migrant. Even if the return is anything but desirable, it is still possible. If it is impossible, then the individual is a refugee. This is why migrants are not eligible for the same kinds of international protections afforded to refugees, especially with regard to admission, settlement, and resettlement in other countries.

Migrant worker — A body on the move looking for, maybe finding, work outside of their country. Often, migrant workers continually move through places and spaces, searching for their next morsel of bread, their next opportunity, temporarily landing here or there, transient, leaving and then returning, or leaving for one place and then leaving from that place to another — a painful, constant mobility. Sometimes, even more painfully, an immobility — the Filipino, Sri Lankan, Ethiopian, and Bengali maids that populate the small pantries off the large kitchens in the homes of wealthy (and sometimes not-so-wealthy) families in other countries;[16] the Indian, Pakistani, and Egyptian day laborers that crowd their streets. Their stays, while transient in the grand scheme of things, are sometimes longer than any human can imagine — decades pass without a return to families or children left behind small and who grow up knowing their mother or father only as a monthly wire transfer.

Immigrant — A migrant who has stayed. As we can see, there is a common thread — a migrating body is on the move because it does not have everything it needs where it is: resources, community, opportunities, a future. A migrating body permanently landing into place is called — from the perspective of the receiving country — an *im*migrant. From the perspective of the leaving country, an *e*migrant. The leaving and receiving shape our understanding of that migration.

Expatriate — White immigrants. This particular term is interesting because it throws into sharp relief the racialization of the term *immigrant* in the current political moment. Growing up in Jordan, I met many American and British citizens living there, sometimes for their whole lives. They never referred to themselves as immigrants. We never referred to them as immigrants. Immigrants are brown and Black bodies moving into white spaces. Expatriates are white bodies moving into brown and Black spaces. Expatriates are ideologically conceptualized as those who bring with them good things, prestige, to their new home. Immigrants are ideologically conceptualized as those who need things from their new home. Neither of these ideological conceptualizations is objective, transparent, or true.

Irregular migration — A rupture in the normal flow of mobility from one place to another. Irregular migration usually involves larger numbers of unwelcome people. The terms do not intend to be racist, but they do reflect racist responses to moving bodies, which are deemed "irregular" when the movement is from south to north, from east to west, and from brown and Black to white-dominant communities, especially en masse — urgent and pressing. We have called similar movements (in the reverse) Manifest Destiny and Empire. Irregular migration could be conflated with "illegal" migration given the statement by the UN: "States are entitled to take measures to prevent irregular border crossings."[17] While movement is irregular (read illegal), the right to seek asylum is universal, and hence irregular can be regularized through the process of seeking asylum.

Large movements — Significant movement of large groups of people who might be moving for different reasons (by force or by choice) but using the same routes of travel (especially by land and water).

Internally displaced — On the verge of refugeedom. Separated from it sometimes by less than a mile, these are bodies seeking asylum with their kinfolk, their country folk, within their country's borders. They have not yet crossed a national border. There are many Palestinian refugees who have left 1948 Israeli-occupied territory and currently live in Palestinian territories and Gaza.[18] As with all other forms of displacements, you can be internally displaced for decades and generations.

Undocumented — In the American context, the term refers to an individual who has entered the US through either legal means (some kind of visa) or "illegal" means (crossing borders without presenting oneself to the authorities to seek asylum) and does not currently have the necessary paperwork to allow them to remain in the country. There are eleven million "undocumented" individuals in the US.[19] It is important to note the problematic usage of the term. Not until very recently (in the scope of human history) could a person be any other kind of immigrant. All bodies on the move were "undocumented." For example, when the English Puritans landed on Plymouth Rock, the local Native populations did not ask for their documentation proving that they had come to settle legally. The need for documentation occurred when borders were created to demarcate and separate geographically delineated areas from each other, and when crossing those borders became a political act with political consequences. Documentation, and the need for it, has more to do with the place and its politics than it does with the individual. And of course, what we think of as undocumented in the here and now (twentieth- and twenty-first-century America) is informed by the politics around immigration from South and Latin America. Looked at another way, we can say that all humans are, in one way or another, documented — many have birth certificates or are recorded in birth registries, someone witnessed their entrance into the world and marked it — somehow, in some way. They have papers that show they belong to a particular country or nation. Thus, in this particular case, "undocumented" says more about American politics than it does about a body defined by absence, by lack.

DACAmented — *DACA* is an acronym for "Deferred Action for Childhood Arrivals." Many children crossed the United States' southern border with their parents who came to the US for safety, security, or better economic opportunity. Some of these children were, sadly, old enough to remember the harrowing journey, perhaps with a coyote (smuggler), perhaps by themselves, across treacherous terrain and in the face of dangerous obstacles (human and natural); they still carry the trauma with them.[20] But many of them were infants and toddlers, too young to even remember a home other than the United States. Deportation for them is the cruelest of jokes — to what would they be returning? They do not know the language, the people, the place to which they would be deported. There are many rules governing eligibility for DACA, such as age, time in this country, crime record, and student or service history. For example, under the DACA program, an individual who came to the US (and has been here since 2007) when they were younger than sixteen years old (and are currently under forty years old) may apply for and receive a two-year postponement of deportation with the ability to renew. To be eligible for DACA, they must have committed no recorded crime. They must be a student or have graduated high school or be a veteran. DACA is not a lawful status; DACA is the temporary postponement of deportation. DACA is a waiting room filled with anxiety and fear. DACA means that you watch as your parents are deported, passing through the doors in the waiting room before you do.

Deportation — The forcible removal of a person from their current country of residence (by that country's government) to their (perceived) country of origin. An additional displacement.[21]

Diaspora — The fragmentation of a people into the world beyond their country of origin. I am part of the Palestinian diaspora. There are more of us outside historical Palestine than inside it.[22] For the descendants of Palestinian refugees (who are also considered refugees) born in, living in the diaspora, what would the UNHCR's durable solutions for refugees — "repatriation, reintegration, rehabilitation and reconstruction" — look like? Like the DACAmented, our homeland is a specter, and we are its specters.

Resettlement — Something that rarely happens to refugees. Most refugees escape the conflict zone quickly, with urgency. The bombs are falling *now*. And if not now, then any second, any minute, any hour, any day. Refugees have seen what has happened to their family members or their next-door neighbors; they have heard what has happened in the village just on the other side of the hill. They must not — cannot — wait any longer. They take what they can — only what can be carried on foot, in overcrowded cars and trucks, in dinghies not meant for anything other than calm waters — and seek safety in the countries right next door that are often under-resourced and impoverished, "underdeveloped" or developing, and often only a trip wire away from exploding themselves.[23] There they languish in stateless limbo, sometimes for generations,[24] because the situations that produce refugees are usually protracted and unsolved, and the return is rarely possible. The world's richest countries take in the least number of refugees; many of them take in none at all.[25] Even at the height of the United States' Refugee

Admissions Program, the US annually resettled less than 1 percent of the world's twenty-six million refugees.

What happens to the majority of the world's refugees is akin to "settling" rather than "resettling" — there is no intentional integration into the community, no rights and privileges granted, no work authorization, no health insurance, no formalized access to public health services, no citizenship, no residential status. Ghosts, specters, they live "under the table" in basements, in tents that morph into zinc-roofed boxes, in dilapidated rooms, and slowly, over time, their shape solidifies, but only just.

Stateless — A person too long unsettled, who neither belongs to the place they left nor belongs to the place they are now. Unclaimed by any country. A citizen of nowhere. An unsettled refugee.[26]

Although we ought not to conflate *refugee* with *asylum seeker* with *undocumented* with *stateless* with *migrant* — their reasons for leaving vary, and the routes they choose also vary — they have much in common.

They often take great risks on their journey — with their own lives and the lives of those who depend on them.

Many do not survive the perilous journey — they drown, asphyxiate, freeze, starve, are murdered along the way.

Many contract life-threatening illnesses and infections.

Many pay smugglers or coyotes to increase their chances of making it.

Many are betrayed by these traffickers.

Along the way, many are assaulted. Many are abused. Many are raped. Impregnated. Kidnapped. Trafficked. Enslaved. Sold. Bought. Women and children are particularly vulnerable.

Many are unaccompanied minors. Many are old or disabled.

Many are children who miss years of schooling and healthy socialization.

Many are criminalized, detained, imprisoned, killed.

Most are unwelcome at various ports of arrival. Most are ghettoized upon arrival. Their descendants are born into statelessness or generational poverty.

These different terms are not necessarily defining fundamentally *different* people; instead, they reflect the contested human body on the move, defined and redefined by observing, releasing, and receiving communities, organizations, and authorities.

They are spectral not only because they are made invisible, ghost-like, consolidated into unimaginable numbers that translate into easily disposable bodies, but also because their rights are on a spectrum, at the whim of the borders they cross, the states they inhabit, the laws they collide with, the ideologies that overdetermine their fate.

International and national laws say a human body on the move has rights — but those rights are nothing in the face of the prejudices encountered along the way.

The internally displaced *could* become asylum seekers *could* become refugees *could* become resettled — but more likely they *become* undocumented *become* stateless *become* unsettled.

By the Numbers

The US has received very high numbers of migrants not born on its soil — those who migrated by force or by choice. It has been a refuge to many escaping religious and ethnic persecution, especially from European countries. And it has also been a hellscape for those brought here against their will — the millions of enslaved Africans[27] (and their descendants for whom the legacy of slavery is a living and breathing reality) and many others it has exploited to work on building its infrastructure but excluded for a long time from its benefits, such as Chinese railroad workers.[28] Refugee resettlement, however, is a fairly recent phenomenon. Refugees were acknowledged and defined by the United Nations as in need of international protection and "durable solutions" after the massive forced migration exodus of World War II. In 1951, the Geneva Convention established the Office of the United Nations High Commissioner for Refugees and declared refugees as people who can prove that they are not able to return to their country for fear of death or persecution based on specific reasons. Since 1951, refugees have found their way to the United States, admitted through a variety of acts related to refugees and displaced individuals.

According to a report by the Center for Migration Studies and Refugee Council USA released in December 2020, the US admitted nearly 1.3 million refugees[29] and asylees between 1945 and 1980, when the Refugee Act was passed, establishing the US refugee resettlement program as it exists today and known as US Refugee Admissions Program (USRAP). Since 1980, the US has resettled more than 3.1 million refugees,* far more than any other country.[30] Crucial here is the understanding of the term *resettlement*, which means organized governmental and local support for integration of lawfully admitted refugees and asylum seekers. Many countries have absorbed many more refugees from neighboring countries during conflict, but those refugees would not be considered "resettled."

The highest refugee admissions to the US since the passage of the act were in 1980 and 1981.[31] Our other high admission numbers were in '89 through '95, and 2008 through 2016 — under an even representation of Republican and Democratic administrations. Since 1981, however, annual refugee admission has never gone above 150,000 and, since 1995, never above 100,000. The lowest numbers of admissions thus far have been during the Trump administration — with historic lows in 2018 and then the lowest of all in 2020.[32]

* https://www.state.gov/refugee-admissions/.

These numbers and demographics tell a story about the US and its policies of hospitality and hostility, as well as a story of its relationships to conflicts around the world. For example, our role in Vietnam as well as the conflicts in Cambodia and elsewhere show our hospitality toward nationals from those regions during the early '80s. Over that decade, hospitality was also extended to refugees from the former Soviet Union.

Into the '90s, we received refugees from Europe, Africa, and Near East countries (again, reflecting the history of conflicts in Bosnia, Rwanda, and Iran). Our refugee admissions plummeted in 2002 and 2003 (easily recognizable as a response to September 11) and then again under the Trump administration, which publicly espoused and fomented xenophobic rhetoric that equated Muslim immigrants and refugees with terrorists. In both of those cases, it is not a coincidence that the historic lows in refugee admissions happened around a time of intense anti-Muslim sentiments and explain why refugees are often associated with Muslim or brown people when, in fact, they come from all around the globe. The Trump administration instituted the "Muslim Ban" in January 2017, which prevented refugee admission and immigration from several Muslim countries on the premise that they were likely terrorists. These conflations exacerbate the myths and misunderstandings about immigrants and refugees.

The process of refugee admission to the US is complex, and it involves a variety of national and multinational stakeholders. Each year, the US president makes a determination about how many refugees, and from which countries, should be admitted for resettlement. This determination is arrived at after consultation with Congress and others and takes into consideration humanitarian needs on the international scene. While the particular conflicts and crises around the world play a big role in this determination, the process also gives deference to nationals whose personal relationship with the

US, usually through a presence of US military and other government personnel in their country, places them in jeopardy. Such
people may be granted a Special Immigrant Visa and have included
Vietnamese and Iraqi nationals who provided support — anything
from translation work to menial labor — and may be regarded by
their countrymen as collaborators or traitors.

It usually takes up to two years from the moment someone is
designated as a refugee by the UNHCR to be, if they are incredibly
lucky, resettled in the US.

For those who are lucky enough to be resettled, it is almost
always after a long and arduous process of screening, review,
and vetting in second countries by international contractors and
US agencies.[33] As previously explained, those lucky enough to
be approved for travel to the US must pay back the cost of their
transport a few months after their arrival, something possibly
doable for those traveling alone or small families, but unimagin-
ably expensive for large families.[34] When refugees are approved
for admission, a consultation with the various volags (nine officially designated refugee resettlement "voluntary agencies" in the
US) determines where in the US they should go based on potential for reunification with family members already in the US, the
suitability of particular refugee populations to particular locations
(is there an existing community, an infrastructure for that group,
resources, opportunities, and the like?), and local capacity. Once
refugees arrive, they receive support through the refugee resettlement agency, which uses the refugee's onetime stipend to secure
housing and other material needs and to provide case management
around health, human, and social services. Refugee support in the
US, especially at the level of local refugee resettlement agencies,
non-profit organizations, and service providers, includes many
former refugees whose intimate knowledge of the experience as
well as cultural and linguistic skills make them a natural fit for this
effort. Many former refugees feel that they would like to improve

the resettlement experience and give back to their new communities and its newest members.[35]

Already underfunded, understaffed, and under-resourced, local resettlement agencies suffered cuts under the Trump administration. The CMS/USRAP reported that "since 2017, the number of local resettlement agencies has fallen from roughly 325 to 200 offices" and that the remaining offices have lost funding and staff, heavily affecting the quality, nature, breadth, and depth of their work.

The effect is not simply material. It is also emotional, social, and ideological. Refugees in the US recognize the maligning false myths that circulate about them. They know that many consider them to be terrorists, parasites, and job takers. And even more sadly, that they have left their countries by choice and are uneducated and unskilled. As we have seen, such beliefs could not be further from the truth. Refugees leave by force because they are escaping death, and once they arrive, material support is limited. Refugees are expected under the guidelines of the current reception and placement expectations to achieve self-sufficiency within ninety days of their arrival; they almost always have to, indeed are told to, accept the first job they are offered.[36] Often, these are jobs most Americans do not want — in food processing and packaging plants — and are almost always menial and completely unrelated to the individual's skills, passions, knowledge, and certification. Refugees, and it is sad that it bears repeating, are simply *people who had to leave their country*. They could be anybody — janitors, doctors, artists, professors, engineers, construction workers, shopkeepers, tailors, chefs, farmers. And while they might depend on public resources and public benefits initially, they are no parasites. Indeed, research shows that refugees overtake natives in contributing to economic growth.[37]

The USRAP's expectation that refugees achieve speedy — one might say untenable — financial independence prevents most refugees from having the time and space to integrate into their local communities, become fluent in English, take care of their children, afford safe housing, pursue desirable employment or educational opportunities, and thrive. Because economic self-sufficiency does not mean integration, many refugees simply survive. When we compare America's refugee reception with those in other countries offering resettlement, the differences are stark.[38] The many gaps left by the program — in funding, housing, childcare, health access, language training access, integration support, and employment support — have necessitated the proliferation of local community resources and organizations. In Greensboro, for example, a mid-sized city of three hundred thousand people, myriad organizations and community groups, other than the refugee resettlement agencies proper, have been founded over the years — the New Arrivals Institute, UNCG's Center for New North Carolinians, FaithAction International House, Islamic Relief USA, and more. So, while refugee resettlement in the US happens formally through collaborations among the Department of State, Office of Refugee Resettlement (ORR), UNHCR, and local refugee resettlement agencies, the great need on the ground for the humane integration of traumatized individuals who have lost everything and with limited language proficiency has given rise to community intervention. This is why myths about the lavish resources, funding, and opportunities available to refugees are particularly cruel and could not be further from the truth. The current Reception and Placement Program, sans community intervention, does not allow people to thrive, and economic self-sufficiency involves many key factors that need to be more fully supported by the program (childcare, transportation, English proficiency, mental health support, et cetera).

Given America's narrative about itself, the level of animosity toward refugees is surprising seeing as they are a group closely aligned with that narrative. Refugees are individuals seeking freedom from persecution; their tenacity and resilience is evidenced by the grueling journey they have endured to arrive safely here. They love their families above all else; indeed, many refugees risk their lives to give their children a better one. And most important, they are incredibly hardworking; there is nothing easy about becoming a refugee to begin with, but they also contribute to the economic well-being and development of the communities in which they resettle. They are the most likely to open small businesses and stimulate abandoned towns, for example.[39] The disconnect between generalized animosity *toward* refugees and idealized values represented *by* refugees suggests that the issue is significantly racialized. Freedom, independence, resilience, and family-orientedness are valued when associated with particular racial groups deemed to be the "good immigrants," the "good refugees." Black and brown refugees, on the other hand, are not assumed to be good. They are "bad" until they prove otherwise — which sometimes takes superhuman effort.

Indeed, Black and brown refugees and migrants are so dehumanized that far too often any support is considered too much. And only *super*human refugees are considered worthy of "human" status. In 2018, for example, a Malian migrant in France, Mamoudou Gassama, scaled a building to save a dangling four-year-old boy.[40] President Macron presented him with French citizenship in acknowledgment of his Spider Man–like action.[41]

Three years previously, it was another little old boy who also managed to humanize the face of the refugee crisis for many of us, achieved only again by his transcendence from mere human status — his death. In 2015, the world's heart broke when images of Alan Kurdi, a Syrian boy traveling with his mother and brother by dinghy, was found on the shores of a resort town in Turkey, drowned. Both his mother and younger brother had also drowned, but there was something about the way in which Alan was found and photographed — gently laid out on the sand on his stomach, the way a toddler would sleep, unblemished, unbruised, eyes closed, fair — that put a superhuman (because angelic) face on the staggering number of Syrian refugees and those who are perishing in perilous sea crossings.[42] And all of a sudden, because Alan became human, we saw him as one of our own — our own daughter or son, asleep on their stomach in their bed — just like Macron saw Gassama as one of his own, a French citizen.

For us in the US, as it did around the world, Alan's humanizing death mobilized incredible interest in and support for refugee communities. Many national and international organizations and initiatives supporting refugees were founded in 2015, including my own, Every Campus A Refuge.

However, soon after, Trump was elected president. Anti-immigrant and anti-refugee rhetoric and policies defined his candidacy and fueled his campaign. As soon as he was inaugurated, he instituted the "Muslim Ban."

Since then, harm to refugee resettlement in the US has extended well beyond the historic dips in refugee admissions. The Trump administration's policies decimated the existing federal and private infrastructure; a number of resettlement agencies closed or laid off staff, resulting in USRAP's "loss in expertise, institutional knowledge, language diversity, and resettlement capacity."[43] The decrease in admissions, as well as process and policy change, "have also badly damaged the community-based infrastructures and networks."[44] These took decades to establish and have "successfully settled and helped integrate more than 3 million refugees, extended services to countless members of host communities, and revitalized many communities."[45] Trump's decision making around refugee admissions also flouted the usual process of consulting with Congress and stakeholders while simultaneously giving states and localities the right to veto refugee resettlement within their jurisdiction. In fact, Executive Order 13888 takes that a step further by necessitating the procurement of written "consent" from localities that want to resettle refugees. Under Trump, the US opposed the Global Compact on Refugees adopted by the UN and affirmed by an overwhelming majority of nations.

The current administration, Joe Biden's, faces the arduous task of rebuilding the refugee resettlement program as the number of refugee admissions is expected to increase significantly over the coming years.[46]

Regardless of the larger national and international policies and laws, local community support for resettling refugees will always be of critical importance. Every Campus A Refuge believes that colleges and universities can be effective receiving communities and play a pivotal role in successful refugee resettlement. Campuses can provide housing, utilities, and use of facilities, amenities, and resources (classes, gym, library, career center, cafeteria, and more), all for free. These resources can be aligned with the hosted guests' passions and interests so that they might thrive rather than simply survive. Blaise's love for music and guitar found expression in jam sessions with faculty and students in the music department; Jacob's (Jennifer's brother) love for soccer was fed with the International Student Club's pickup games; Ali's love of art found a home in the art department, with its private studios and supplies. Our volunteers rallied around our guests, providing them with airport welcomes, preparing the house for their arrival, raising and collecting funds and in-kind donations, sharing meals, acting as cultural brokers, providing interpretation, making appointments, looking after children, job hunting, shopping, and so much more. And when families moved off campus, we stayed connected and supportive.

My Palestinian parents and grandparents' experiences in Jordan — where difference was emphasized, belonging was elusive, and "home" was never found — undergirds the ethos of Every Campus A Refuge. The "ivory tower" exclusivity of college and university campuses is fundamentally upended so that the newcomers' belonging rather than their difference is centralized, and the campus we speak of and imagine as safe for those who traditionally "belong" there is also safe for other new members of our community who *need* to be there, at least for a short while.

Although I initially modeled Every Campus A Refuge on the pope's call for radical hospitality, over the years I have come to see it also as a call for radical accountability.

Institutions of higher learning do not simply teach their students. They model for their larger communities what "community" ought to be. And they acknowledge that they are part of systems that ought not to be and ought never to have been.

I was always proud of Guilford College's legacy and felt that Every Campus A Refuge was a natural extension of the institution's role in the Underground Railroad in which the nearby Quakers provided sustenance to the escaping slaves, who were hiding in trees' expansive roots, and smuggled them up north.[47]

However, Guilford College did not admit Black students until 1962.[48] And like every other institution of higher education on this continent, it is built on lands that belonged to indigenous tribes. The college is also part of a country whose wealth is built on the labor of African enslaved people, a forced migration of epic proportions and enduring legacies of pain. And it is part of a country whose international exploits and interventions have created currents of forced migration around the world, displacing peoples once indigenous elsewhere.

American college and university campuses are at the locus of these international presents and futures, accountable to their indigenous pasts.

We ought to do this work of radical hospitality and radical accountability not simply because we can, but because we *must*.

NOTES

Author's Note

1. The refugee crisis after World War II was in Europe. And throughout the decades since, there have been many other refugees from European countries. For the current number of European refugees, see "UNHCR: Refugee Statistics," United Nations High Commissioner for Refugees, https://www.unhcr.org/refugee-statistics/, accessed July 27, 2021.

Chapter 1: Radical Hospitality

1. Walter R. Erdelen and Jacques G. Richardson, "Human Migration: Managing Its Increasing Complexity," *Foresight* 22, no. 1 (January 1, 2019): 109–26.
2. An Arabic expression translated literally into the English. The Arabic شد الرحال signifies both journeying only with that which can travel or be carried as well as a more specific Islamic usage based on a hadith in which the prophet enjoins that travel should only take place to three mosques, one of them in Jerusalem (Sahih Al-Bukhari 1189).
3. Amir Cheshin, Bill Hutman, and Avi Melamed, *Separate and Unequal* (Cambridge, Mass.: Harvard University Press, 2009), 201.
4. For an analysis of the study of place-naming and examples of this phenomenon, see Reuben Rose-Redwood, Derek Alderman, and Maoz Azaryahu, "Geographies of Toponymic Inscription: New Directions in Critical Place-Name Studies," *Progress in Human Geography* 34, no. 4 (2010): 453–70.
5. The narratives around the "good" and "bad" refugee or immigrant are fomented by anti-immigrant and anti-refugee pundits and cause a great deal of harm.
6. Deir Yassin was the site of a massacre in 1948.
7. Steven Salaita's work often compares the ways in which Anglo-Saxon migration to and through North America (Manifest Destiny and white settler colonialism) is twin to Jewish migration to and through Palestine (Zionism) — both informed by Judeo-Christian white supremacist ideologies of domination. See especially *Holy Land in Transit: Colonialism and the Quest for Canaan* (Syracuse, N.Y.: Syracuse University Press, 2006).
8. Palestinian American artist Leila Abdelrazaq's "A Map of Palestine" shows where the Palestinian diaspora lives all over the world; see https://lalaleila

.com/A-Map-of-Palestine. Large Palestinian communities live in Chile, the US, and Sweden, among others.

9. I detail this experience in "'And Is It Impossible to Be Good Everywhere?': Love and Badness in America and the Arab World," in *Bad Girls of the Arab World*, ed. Rula Quawas and Nadia Yaqub (Austin: University of Texas Press, 2017), 37–48. Reprinted in *Paris Review*, October 2, 2017, https://www.theparisreview.org/blog/2017/10/02/love-and-badness-in-america-and-the-arab-world/.

10. Bryan Walsh and Time Photo, "Alan Kurdi's Story: Behind the Most Heartbreaking Photo of 2015," *Time*, December 29, 2015, time.com/4162306/alan-kurdi-syria-drowned-boy-refugee-crisis.

11. See Emma F. Thomas, Laura G. E. Smith, Craig McGarty, Gerhard Reese, Anna Kende, Ana-Maria Bliuc, Nicola Curtin, and Russell Spears, "When and How Social Movements Mobilize Action Within and Across Nations to Promote Solidarity with Refugees," *European Journal of Social Psychology* 49, no. 2 (2019): 213–29, https://doi.org/10.1002/ejsp.2380; F. Vis and O. Goriunova, eds., *The Iconic Image on Social Media: A Rapid Research Response to the Death of Aylan Kurdi* (Visual Social Media Lab, 2015); and Paul Slovic et al., "Iconic Photographs and the Ebb and Flow of Empathic Response to Humanitarian Disasters," *Proceedings of the National Academy of Sciences* 114, no. 4 (2017): 640–44, doi:10.1073/pnas.1613977114.

12. "Migrant Crisis: Austria to Let People in from Hungary." *BBC News*, September 5, 2015, www.bbc.com/news/world-europe-34159780.

13. Isla Binnie, "Pope Calls on Every European Parish to Host One Refugee Family," Reuters, September 6, 2015, www.reuters.com/article/us-europe-migrants-pope/pope-calls-on-every-european-parish-to-host-one-refugee-family-idUSKCN0R60DZ20150906.

14. North Carolina is second only to New York in refugee resettlement on the eastern seaboard. Annually, North Carolina welcomes 4 percent of the refugee arrivals to the US ("Archives," Refugee Processing Center, https://www.wrapsnet.org/archives/), and its third largest city of Greensboro welcomes nearly a third of those. Before the Trump administration, the state welcomed on average three thousand refugees annually, with a third of them resettling in Guilford County where Greensboro is the major city.

15. Richard Kearney and Melissa Fitzpatrick, *Radical Hospitality: From Thought to Action* (New York: Fordham University Press, 2021).

Chapter 2: The Body Leaves Its Soul Behind

1. Saudi poet. My translation from the Arabic.

2. I came to the United States for the first time in 1996 as an international student on an F-1 visa. I returned to Jordan to teach in 2003, much to my grandmother's joy. After a conflict with my institution over a freedom of speech

issue, I returned to the US in 2008. I had been naturalized as an American citizen in 2005 through marriage.

3. Peter Gatrell, *The Making of the Modern Refugee* (Oxford, UK: Oxford University Press, 2015), 125.

4. It is also the number of days other prophets spent in crucial locations — the Musa on Mount Sinai, Yunus in the whale, et cetera.

5. An apartheid wall built by the Israeli government in 2002.

6. International Organization of Migration. Established in 1951, it is the "leading inter-governmental organization in the field of migration and works closely with governmental, intergovernmental and non-governmental partners." "About IOM," IOM UN Immigration, https://www.iom.int/about-iom, accessed August 12, 2021. Most refugees travel to their country of resettlement with support from IOM.

Chapter 3: Proof and Persecution

1. To be recognized as a refugee with access to assistance, an individual must prove that they are not able to return to "their country of origin owing to a well-founded fear of being persecuted for reasons of race, religion, nationality, membership of a particular social group, or political opinion." "Convention and Protocol Relating to the Status of Refugees," United Nations High Commissioner for Refugees, December 2010, www.unhcr.org/3b66c2aa10 .html.

2. See "Procedural Standards for Refugee Status Determination Under UNHCR's Mandate," United Nations High Commissioner for Refugees, 2020, www.unhcr .org/4317223c9.pdf; *UNHCR Resettlement Handbook*, United Nations High Commissioner for Refugees, 2011, www.unhcr.org/46f7c0ee2.pdf; Helen Nianias, "Verifying Refugees' Stories: Why Is It so Difficult?" *Guardian*, October 6, 2017, www.theguardian.com/global-development-professionals-network/2016/ nov/17/verifying-refugees-stories-why-is-it-so-difficult; and "Infographic: The Screening Process for Refugee Entry into the United States," whitehouse.gov, November 20, 2015, obamawhitehouse.archives.gov/blog/2015/11/20/infographic -screening-process-refugee-entry-united-states.

3. For various conflicts and wars in Burundi and Congo during this time period, see Sezai Özçelik, "Burundi: Capturing the Complexity of the Conflict in the 1990s," *Conflict Studies Quarterly* 19 (April 2017): 43–64; and Emizet François Kisangani, *Civil Wars in the Democratic Republic of Congo, 1960–2010* (Boulder, Colo.: Lynne Rienner Publishers, 2012).

4. See *UNHCR Resettlement Handbook*, United Nations High Commissioner for Refugees, 2011, www.unhcr.org/46f7c0ee2.pdf, for details and further reading suggestions on why delays in resettlement happen and how family unification and reunification for refugees are challenges.

---

5. For an overview of LGBTQ rights issue in Uganda, see Susan Dicklitch-Nelson, "Are LGBTQ Human Rights in Uganda a Lost Cause?," *Georgetown Journal of International Affairs*, February 27, 2020.

6. "Where We Work," United Nations Relief and Works Agency, www.unrwa.org/where-we-work, accessed August 9, 2021.

7. Marcel was recently approved by the UN, but he still needs to find a country that will resettle him. When he gets to that stage of country selection, he might be asked if he has contacts in those countries. He could potentially provide Cheps's contact information and be resettled in Greensboro.

8. For an overview of the wars in Iraq, see Andrew T. Parasiliti, "The Causes and Timing of Iraq's Wars: A Power Cycle Assessment," *International Political Science Review / Revue Internationale de Science Politique* 24, no. 1 (2003): 151–65; and "War in Iraq: Political Challenges After the Conflict," International Crisis Group, https://www.crisisgroup.org/middle-east-north-africa/gulf-and-arabian-peninsula/iraq/war-iraq-political-challenges-after-conflict, accessed July 28, 2021.

Chapter 4: Right Next Door

1. "Lives in Storage: Refugee Warehousing and the Overlooked Humanitarian Crisis," ReliefWeb, US Committee for Refugees and Immigrants, December 2019.

2. For information about Black September and its effect on Palestinians living in Jordan, see Iris Fruchter-Ronen, "Black September: The 1970–71 Events and Their Impact on the Formation of Jordanian National Identity," *Civil Wars* 10, no. 3 (2008): 244–60; Hassan A. Barari, "Four Decades After Black September: A Jordanian Perspective," *Civil Wars* 10, no. 3 (2008): 231–43; and Barbara Gallets, "Black September and Identity Construction in Jordan," *Journal of Georgetown University–Qatar Middle Eastern Studies Student Association* 1 (2015).

3. For more context and statistics about the Syrian civil war, see Itamar Rabinovich and Carmit Valensi, *Syrian Requiem: The Civil War and Its Aftermath* (Princeton, N.J.: Princeton University Press, 2021), https://uncg.on.worldcat.org/v2/oclc/1152424272; and Statista Research Department, "Topic: The Syrian Civil War," *Statista*, April 1, 2021, www.statista.com/topics/4216/the-syrian-civil-war/#topicHeader__wrapper.

4. United Nations High Commissioner for Refugees, "Inside the World's Five Largest Refugee Camps," USA for UNHCR The Refugee Agency, April 1, 2021, www.unrefugees.org/news/inside-the-world-s-five-largest-refugee-camps.

5. At the time this happened, Um Fihmi was in the US. Our organization was able to intervene and arrange for surgery for Hazar with a well-known children's orthopedist in Jordan. She is now walking normally and still lives in Jordan.

6. Such as the group Refugee Flak Kakuma. For more on experiences of LGBTQ individuals, see "'Go Fund Me': LGBTI Asylum Seekers in Kakuma Refugee Camp, Kenya," in Christine M. Jacobsen et al., *Waiting and the Temporalities of Irregular Migration* (Oxfordshire: Routledge, 2021), 131–48.

7. For more information on the conditions in Kakuma, see Raphael Mweninguwe et al., "Living Conditions in Kenya's Kakuma Refugee Camp Are Harsh and Dangerous," *D+C*, December 18, 2020, www.dandc.eu/en/article/living-conditions-kenyas-kakuma-refugee-camp-are-harsh-and-dangerous.

8. For more information on terrorism in Kenya, see Samuel L. Aronson, "Kenya and the Global War on Terror: Neglecting History and Geopolitics in Approaches to Counterterrorism," *African Journal of Criminology and Justice Studies* 7 (November 2013).

9. Most refugees require such a permit to define their status in the second country. I recall that when we hosted the first Syrian family at Guilford, the father would always bring his right hand to his left shirt pocket, touching it lightly, whenever he saw a car come up the street where they lived on campus. Only the few residents of that remote, dead-end street drove there, and so there were hardly ever any strangers. I never inquired about this. Once, after he made that gesture, unconsciously it seems, he laughed awkwardly at himself when he realized I was there. "Forgive me, uncle," he said. "I am used to having to show my papers. I forgot I don't need them here. I used to keep them in this pocket" — he touched his heart where the papers used to be.

10. Blaise's case took seventeen years to process. It is not something he dwells on or even mentions. I noted it. He told me that he was supposed to make it here sooner, but the war in Burundi and then the ban on refugees interrupted his case.

Chapter 5: Back to the Margins

1. Larisa Epatko, "You Asked: How Are Refugees Referred to Live in the US?," *PBS NewsHour*, March 1, 2017, https://www.pbs.org/newshour/world/asked-refugees-referred-live-u-s.

2. At the time of this writing, this onetime stipend is $1,025.

3. More than two hundred thousand as of this writing. See Statista Research Department, "Topic: The Syrian Civil War," *Statista*, April 1, 2021, www.statista.com/topics/4216/the-syrian-civil-war/#topicHeader_wrapper.

4. See "What Is Cultural Orientation?: Cultural Orientation Resource Exchange," CORE, https://coresourceexchange.org/about-cultural-orientation/, accessed July 21, 2021.

5. "Chapter 2: Adjudicative Factors," US Citizenship and Immigration Services, August 5, 2021, www.uscis.gov/policy-manual/volume-12-part-f-chapter-2.

6. Cheps was our first guest. He was sworn in as an American citizen in a ceremony in Charlotte at the end of June 2021. He is the first ECAR guest to have

been naturalized. This excites him, of course, especially because now he will be able to vote in the presidential elections as a way of expressing his rights as a citizen.

7. Indeed, implicit in that assumption is that living in the US is all one needs to be happy — a Eurocentric/Americentric ideology at the root of much xenophobic discourse, which presumes that simply being in America must be the goal for everybody (especially Black and brown people) who live outside it. At the center of this ideology is the harmful belief that we are the best and that everybody wants to be US, *with* US, *in* US. An extension of that belief is that everything else is worse. And the most harmful extension of that belief is that by default, then, everybody must want to take away from us what we have because it is so much better than what they have. These ideologies are damaging to refugees and undergirded by egotistical concepts about ourselves and dehumanizing beliefs about others.

8. Refugees experience severe mental health issues. See Derrick Silove et al., "The Contemporary Refugee Crisis: An Overview of Mental Health Challenges," *World Psychiatry* 16, no. 2 (2017): 130–39, doi:10.1002/wps.20438.

9. Another example of Guilford's commitment to social justice. A few years back, the highly principled Guilford College students had organized and mobilized to remove the caterer at the time, a corporate one whose treatment of their workers was no better than their food; the caterer was replaced by a worker-friendly, earth-friendly company. The small organization held a few contracts and was committed to green practices, organic food, and labor support.

10. See Hikmet Jamil et al., "Promoters and Barriers to Work: A Comparative Study of Refugees Versus Immigrants in the United States," *New Iraqi Journal of Medicine* 8, no. 2 (2012): 19–28.

11. Qur'an 15:9.

12. Many refugees and immigrants work in food processing plants. See Angela Stuesse and Nathan T. Dollar, "Who Are America's Meat and Poultry Workers?," Economic Policy Institute, September 24, 2020, www.epi.org/blog/meat-and-poultry-worker-demographics/.

13. In the US and elsewhere. See Moira Donovan, "A Persisting Challenge: Housing for Refugees," *US Together*, August 3, 2021, www.ustogether.us/blog/2021/7/22/a-persisting-challenge-housing-for-refugees; and S. Soederberg, "Governing Global Displacement in Austerity Urbanism: The Case of Berlin's Refugee Housing Crisis," *Development and Change* 50 (2019): 923–47, https://doi.org/10.1111/dech.12455.

14. Federal occupancy limit is two per bedroom, which North Carolina follows. Fair Housing Act challenges this. See Lauren Brasil, "Occupancy Policies and the Fair Housing Act: How Many Is Too Many?," Fair Housing Project, December 4, 2018,

https://www.fairhousingnc.org/newsletter/occupancy-policies-and-the-fair-housing-act-how-many-is-too-many/; and Department of Housing and Urban Development, "Fair Housing Enforcement — Occupancy Standards; Statement of Policy; Notice; Republication," *Federal Register* 63, no. 245 (1998), www.fairhousingnc.org/wp-content/uploads/2012/03/HUD-Keating-Memo-on-Occupancy-Standards-3-20-1991.pdf.

15. For news stories about this incident and its aftermath, see Maddie Gardner, "5 Children Die After Greensboro Apartment Fire," wfmynews2.com, May 14, 2018, and David Ford, "Unsafe Haven" 88.5 WFDD, January 3, 2019, https://www.wfdd.org/show/unsafe-haven.

16. See Eva Clark et al., "Disproportionate Impact of the COVID-19 Pandemic on Immigrant Communities in the United States," *PLoS Neglected Tropical Diseases* 14, no. 7 (July 13, 2020): e0008484, doi:10.1371/journal.pntd.0008484; Stefano Scarpetta et al., "What Is the Impact of the COVID-19 Pandemic on Immigrants and Their Children?" *OECD*, October 19, 2020; and Sarah K. Clarke et al., "Potential Impact of COVID-19 on Recently Resettled Refugee Populations in the United States and Canada: Perspectives of Refugee Health-care Providers," *Journal of Immigrant and Minority Health* 23, no. 1 (February 1, 2021): 184–89, https://doi.org/10.1007/s10903-020-01104-4.

Chapter 6: From Camp to Campus

1. Support for resettling refugees varies across resettling countries. See C. M. Lanphier, "Refugee Resettlement: Models in Action," *International Migration Review* 17, no. 1 (1983): 4–33; Katharine M. Donato and Elizabeth Ferris, "Refugee Integration in Canada, Europe, and the United States: Perspectives from Research," *Annals of the American Academy of Political and Social Science* 690, no. 1 (July 2020): 7–35, doi:10.1177/0002716220943169; and Nicole Ostrand, "The Syrian Refugee Crisis: A Comparison of Responses by Germany, Sweden, the United Kingdom, and the United States," *Journal on Migration and Human Security* 3, no. 3 (September 2015): 255–79, doi:10.1177/233150241500300301.

2. Transplanting Traditions Community Farm in North Carolina. Ree Ree has recently been appointed its executive director.

3. There have been many studies on the mental health consequences of forced migration and the high rates of post-traumatic stress disorder and other psychological disorders among refugees, as well as the challenges in addressing those mental health issues. See, for example, Man Cheung Chung et al., "Post-traumatic Stress Among Syrian Refugees: Trauma Exposure Characteristics, Trauma Centrality, and Emotional Suppression," *Psychiatry* 81, no. 1 (2018): 54–70; Ali Zbidat et al., "The Perceptions of Trauma, Complaints, Somatization, and Coping Strategies Among Syrian Refugees in Germany: A Qualitative Study of an At-Risk Population," *International Journal of Environmental*

Research and Public Health 17, no. 3 (2020): 693; Susan S. Y. Li, Belinda J. Liddell, and Angela Nickerson, "The Relationship Between Post-Migration Stress and Psychological Disorders in Refugees and Asylum Seekers," *Current Psychiatry Reports* 18 (2016): 82; Cécile Rousseau, "Addressing Mental Health Needs of Refugees," *Canadian Journal of Psychiatry* 63, no. 5 (May 2018): 287–89, doi:10.1177/0706743717746664; and Silove et al., "The Contemporary Refugee Crisis."

Chapter 7: Names and Numbers

1. P. Douglas, M. Cetron, and P. Spiegel, "Definitions Matter: Migrants, Immigrants, Asylum Seekers and Refugees," *Journal of Travel Medicine* 26, no. 2 (2019).

2. Nando Sigona, "The Contested Politics of Naming in Europe's 'Refugee Crisis,'" *Ethnic and Racial Studies* 41, no. 3 (2018): 456–60.

3. For example for Juana Luz Tobar Ortega, who stayed in sanctuary for four years. See "Asheboro Woman Who Sought Sanctuary in Greensboro Church for 4 Years Granted Stay of Removal by Federal Officials, Returns Home," *Greensboro News and Record*, April 20, 2021, https://greensboro.com/news /local/asheboro-woman-who-sought-sanctuary-in-greensboro-church-for-4 -years-granted-stay-of-removal/article_75ea596a-a201-11eb-adcb 0fae4618d142.html; and Pilar Timpane and Christine Delp, directors, *Santuario*, October 6, 2018, http://www.santuariofilm.com/.

4. Sulayman N. Khalaf, "Settlement of Violence in Bedouin Society," *Ethnology* 29, no. 3 (1990): 225–42, www.jstor.org/stable/3773568, accessed July 7, 2021.

5. "Asylum in the United States," American Immigration Council, February 26, 2021, www.americanimmigrationcouncil.org/research/asylum-united-states.

6. Judith Kumin and Frances Nicholson, *A Guide to International Refugee Protection and Building State Asylum Systems*, Inter-Parliamentary Union and the United Nations High Commissioner for Refugees, 2017, www.unhcr .org/3d4aba564.pdf.

7. For example, incidents where indigenous Native Americans are accused of being "illegal" such as Ben Giles and Paulina Pineda, "Legislative Staffers Say Pro-Trump Supporters Called Them 'Illegal' for Being Dark-Skinned," *Arizona Capitol Times* (blog), January 26, 2018, https://azcapitoltimes.com/ news/2018/01/26/arizona-capitol-eric-descheenie-cesar-chavez-lisette -flores-selianna-robles-katie-hobbs-tomas-robles-trump-supports-yell -illegal/.

8. See Steven Feldstein, "How US Policies Are Worsening the Global Refugee Crisis," Carnegie Endowment for International Peace, https://carnegieendow ment.org/2017/10/16/how-u.s.-policies-are-worsening-global-refugee-crisis -pub-73480, accessed July 29, 2021; Rebecca Gordon, "The Current Migrant Crisis Was Created by US Foreign Policy, Not Trump," *The Nation*, August 16,

2019, www.thenation.com/article/archive/central-america-migrant-crisis-for eign-policy-trump; and Mark Tseng-Putterman, "A Century of US Intervention Created the Immigration Crisis," *Medium*, June 28, 2018, medium.com/s/story/timeline-us-intervention-central-america-a9bea9ebc148.

9. "Asylum and Migration," United Nations High Commissioner for Refugees, www.unhcr.org/en-us/asylum-and-migration.html, accessed August 9, 2021.

10. For a history of the UNHCR, see "History of UNHCR," United Nations High Commissioner for Refugees, 2020, www.unhcr.org/en-us/history-of-unhcr .html; and G. Loescher, "UNHCR's Origins and Early History: Agency, Influence, and Power in Global Refugee Policy," *Refuge* 33, no. 1 (2017): 77–86.

11. "'Refugees' and 'Migrants': Frequently Asked Questions (FAQs)," UN High Commissioner for Refugees, August 31, 2018, https://www.refworld.org/docid/56e81c0d4.html.

12. Camps that are created, usually out of tents, on the periphery of national borders to warehouse refugees. These camps are often large prisons that refugees cannot leave without documentation. For more on such camps, see "Lives in Storage: Refugee Warehousing and the Overlooked Humanitarian Crisis," ReliefWeb, US Committee for Refugees and Immigrants, December 2019, reliefweb.int/sites/reliefweb.int/files/resources/USCRI-Warehousing -Dec2019-v4.pdf.

13. "A person is a refugee because of the lack of protection by their country of origin. Moving to a new country of asylum does not change this, so it does not affect a person's status as a refugee. A person who meets the criteria for refugee status remains a refugee, regardless of the particular route they travel in search of protection or opportunities to rebuild their life, and regardless of the various stages involved in that journey." "'Refugees' and 'Migrants,'" UN High Commissioner for Refugees.

14. And according to UNRWA, Palestinian refugees are defined as "persons whose normal place of residence was Palestine during the period 1 June 1946 to 15 May 1948, and who lost both home and means of livelihood as a result of the 1948 conflict. . . . The descendants of Palestine refugee males, including adopted children, are also eligible for registration. When the Agency began operations in 1950, it was responding to the needs of about 750,000 Palestine refugees. Today, some 5 million Palestine refugees are eligible for UNRWA services." https://www.unrwa.org/palestine-refugees.

15. UN General Assembly, New York Declaration for Refugees and Migrants: Resolution Adopted by General Assembly, October 3, 2016, https://www .refworld.org/docid/57ceb74a4.html.

16. Pei-Chia Lan, "Maid or Madam? Filipina Migrant Workers and the Continuity of Domestic Labor," *Gender & Society* 17, no. 2 (April 2003): 187–208; Pardis Mahdavi, "Gender, Labour and the Law: The Nexus of Domestic Work, Human Trafficking and the Informal Economy in the United Arab Emirates,"

Global Networks 13, no. 4 (2013): 425–40, https://doi.org/10.1111/glob.12010; and Eric Bellman, "Nations Seek Shields for Migrant Workers: Maids' Ranks Swell in Middle East and Asia," *Wall Street Journal* (online), October 2, 2014.

17. UN General Assembly, New York Declaration for Refugees and Migrants.

18. "UNHCR: Refugee Statistics"; and "Palestine," Internal Displacement Monitoring Centre, https://www.internal-displacement.org/countries/Palestine, accessed July 27, 2021. There are also currently 6,568,000 internally displaced Syrians. "Syria," IDMC, https://www.internal-displacement.org/countries/Syria, accessed July 27, 2021.

19. And they come from all over the world, including Europe. See "Mexicans Decline to Less than Half the US Unauthorized Immigrant Population for the First Time," *Pew Research Center* (blog), https://www.pewresearch.org/fact-tank/2019/06/12/us-unauthorized-immigrant-population-2017/, accessed July 27, 2021.

20. See Reina Grande, *The Distance Between Us: A Memoir* (Aladdin Press, 2016).

21. Between 1892 and 2018, nearly 4.6 million people were deported from the US. See Alex Nowrasteh, "Deportation Rates in Historical Perspective," Cato Institute, September 16, 2019, https://www.cato.org/blog/deportation-rates-historical-perspective.

22. Nearly two-thirds of the 11.2 million Palestinian people (as of 2012) are forcibly displaced. See Susan Akram and Nidal Al-Azza, eds., *Closing Protection Gaps: Handbook on Protection of Palestinian Refugees in States Signatories to the 1951 Refugee Convention*, 2nd ed. (al-Ayyam Press, Printing, Publishing & Distribution, 2015), 7, www.badil.org/phocadownloadpap/badil-new/publications/Handbook-art1d/Art1D-2015Handbook.pdf.

23. Seventy-three percent of refugees are hosted in neighboring countries and 86 percent in developing countries. "Figures at a Glance," United Nations High Commissioner for Refugees, June 18, 2021, www.unhcr.org/en-us/figures-at-a-glance.html.

24. See United Nations High Commissioner for Refugees, "Protracted Refugee Situations Explained," USA for UNHCR The Refugee Agency, January 28, 2020, www.unrefugees.org/news/protracted-refugee-situations-explained/#How%20many%20refugees%20are%20living%20in%20protracted%20situations.

25. There is, at present, no equitable sharing among nations and states of the "burden and responsibility" of hosting and resettling refugees. UN General Assembly, New York Declaration for Refugees and Migrants.

26. The 1954 Convention Relating to the Status of Stateless Persons aims to improve the situation of stateless persons and ensure their human rights. "Information and Accession Package: The 1954 Convention Relating to the Status of Stateless Persons and the 1961 Convention on the Reduction of State-

lessness," United Nations High Commissioner for Refugees, 1996, www
.refworld.org/pdfid/3ae6b3350.pdf.

27. "Possibly the best documented and most widely known incidence of large-
scale forced migration experienced in the history of the African continent is
the slave trade. The trans-Atlantic slave trade is unique in the history of forced
migration in terms of its magnitude, the prolonged period of its practice, the
suffering that its victims endured and the profit that it generated which laid the
foundation of the early development of the capitalist world-economy." Egide
Rwamatwara, "Forced Migration in Africa: A Challenge to Development,"
Journal of African Studies 5 (2005): 173–91 (quote on page 178).

28. See "The Chinese Exclusion Act: Chapter 1," *American Experience*, PBS, www
.pbs.org/wgbh/americanexperience/features/chinese-exclusion-act-chapter-1,
accessed August 9, 2021.

29. Immigration and Naturalization Service Statistical Yearbook FY2000.

30. Center for Migration Studies and Refugee Council USA, *Charting a Course to
Rebuild and Strengthen the US Refugee Admissions Program*, December 2020,
https://cmsny.org/wp-content/uploads/2020/12/CMS-and-RCUSA-Report-
Charting-a-Course-to-Rebuild-and Strengthen-the-US-Refugee-Admis
sions-Program.pdf.

31. Over 200,000 refugees were admitted in 1980 and over 150,000 in 1981; the
majority were from East Asia. "Refugee Admissions by Region: Fiscal Year
1975 Through September 30, 2020," Refugee Processing Center, https://www
.wrapsnet.org/documents/Refugee%20Admissions%20by%20Region%20
since%201975%20as%20of%2010-5-20.pdf.

32. "Refugee Admissions by Region Since 1975 as of September 30, 2020," Refugee
Processing Center, https://www.wrapsnet.org/documents/Refugee%20Adm
issions%20by%20Region%20since%201975%20as%20of%2010-5-20.pdf and
migrationpolicy.org, accessed July 27, 2021; "US Annual Refugee Resettlement
Ceilings and Number of Refugees Admitted, 1980–Present," August 13, 2013,
https://www.migrationpolicy.org/programs/data-hub/charts/us-annual
-refugee-resettlement-ceilings-and-number-refugees-admitted-united.

33. "Infographic: The Screening Process for Refugee Entry into the United States."

34. ECAR once hosted an eleven-member family who had to pay back over
$10,000 in airfare bringing them to this country as refugees.

35. Donald Kerwin and Mike Nicholson, "Charting a Course to Rebuild and
Strengthen the US Refugee Admissions Program (USRAP): Findings and
Recommendations from the Center for Migration Studies Refugee Resettlement Survey: 2020," *Journal on Migration and Human Security* 9, no. 1 (March
2021): 1–30, doi:10.1177/2331502420985043.

36. Indeed, this language is used expressly by refugee resettlement agency case-
workers and staff (for a living example, see the documentary about Syrian

refugees resettling in Baltimore, *This Is Home*, directed by Alexandra Shiva, 2018).

37. "Immigrants as Economic Contributors: Refugees Are a Fiscal Success Story for America," *National Immigration Forum*, November 5, 2018, immigration forum.org/article/immigrants-as-economic-contributors-refugees-are-a -fiscal-success-story-for-america; "From Struggle to Resilience: The Economic Impact of Refugees in America," *New American Economy*, June 2017, http://research.newamericaneconomy.org/wp-content/uploads/sites/2/2017/11/NAE_Refugees_V6.pdf; and Donald Kerwin, "The US Refugee Resettlement Program — A Return to First Principles: How Refugees Help to Define, Strengthen, and Revitalize the United States," *Journal on Migration and Human Security* 6, no. 3 (2018): 1–21.

38. For example, the Canadian model promotes private sponsorship, which should "provide basic assistance such as accommodation, food, and help to find a job, usually for one year after arrival." Ian van Haren, "Canada's Private Sponsorship Model Represents a Complementary Pathway for Refugee Resettlement," Migration Policy Institute, July 9, 2021, www.migrationpolicy.org/article/canada-private-sponsorship-model-refugee-resettlement.

39. Dan Kosten, "Immigrants as Economic Contributors: Immigrant Entrepreneurs," *National Immigration Forum*, November 5, 2018, immigrationforum.org/article/immigrants-as-economic-contributors-immigrant-entrepreneurs; and "From Struggle to Resilience: The Economic Impact of Refugees in America," *New American Economy*, June 2017, http://research.newamericaneconomy.org/wp-content/uploads/sites/2/2017/11/NAE_Refugees_V6.pdf.

40. Aurelien Breeden and Alan Cowell, "Paris 'Spider-Man' Saves Young Boy. Cue Debate on Migrants," *New York Times*, May 28, 2018, www.nytimes.com/2018/05/28/world/europe/paris-migrant-hero-spiderman.html.

41. "I dream of a country where it wouldn't be necessary to scale a building to save the life of a child, at the risk of one's own life, to be treated like a human being when you are a migrant," said Raphaël Glucksmann in a post on Facebook. Raphaël Glucksmann, Opinion on Mamoudou Gassama's Bravery, Facebook, May 28, 2018, https://www.facebook.com/raphael.glucksmann/posts/10155273242237175, accessed August 9, 2021.

42. Visual and Data Journalism Team, "Hundreds of Migrants Still Dying in Med Five Years Since 2015," BBC, September 1, 2020, www.bbc.com/news/world-europe-53764449.

43. Center for Migration Studies and Refugee Council USA, *Charting a Course*, 7.

44. Center for Migration Studies and Refugee Council USA, *Charting a Course*, 12.

45. Center for Migration Studies and Refugee Council USA, *Charting a Course*, 12.

46. Mica Rosenberg and Steve Holland, "Heeding Complaints, Biden Lifts Refugee Cap to 62,500," Reuters, May 3, 2021, www.reuters.com/world/us/
biden-heeds-complaints-lifts-refugee-cap-62500-2021-05-03.

47. Lauren Barber, "An Underground Railroad Station Emerges Near Guilford
College," *Triad City Beat*, February 15, 2019, triad-city-beat.com/an
-underground-railroad-station-emerges-near-guilford-college.

48. Gwen Gosney Erikson, "Race Relations at Guilford College," UNC Greensboro Digital Collections, libcdm1.uncg.edu/cdm/essayguilford/collection/
CivilRights, accessed August 9, 2021.

ACKNOWLEDGMENTS

Thank you to Philip Lentz and Kathleen Herbst for reading early versions of the book and offering support and suggestions. Deep gratitude to Cheps, Blaise, Ree Ree, Marwa, Ali, Um Fihmi, and my mother who entrusted me with their stories. And thank you to everyone at Guilford College who could have easily said "no" and instead said "YES" to becoming a campus refuge.

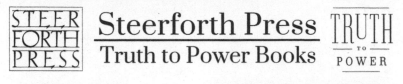

Steerforth Press
Truth to Power Books

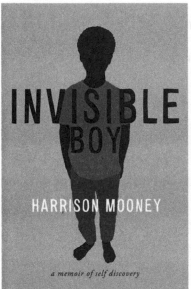

INVISIBLE BOY

HARRISON MOONEY

a memoir of self discovery

I CAN TAKE IT FROM HERE

A MEMOIR
OF TRAUMA,
PRISON,
AND SELF-EMPOWERMENT

LISA FORBES

HOW FREE SPEECH SAVED DEMOCRACY

The Untold History of How the First Amendment Became an Essential Tool for Securing Liberty and Social Justice

Christopher M. Finan
Executive Director of the National Coalition Against Censorship
FOREWORD BY RANDALL KENNEDY

"A gripping, moving tale."
— EVAN THOMAS, AUTHOR OF *IKE'S BLUFF*

IKE'S MYSTERY MAN
THE SECRET LIVES OF ROBERT CUTLER

The Cold War, the Lavender Scare, and the Untold Story of Eisenhower's First National Security Advisor

PETER SHINKLE

FOREWORD BY
CHARLES KAISER

Steerforth Press
Truth to Power Books

TRUTH TO **POWER**

THE WOMAN WHO INSPIRED
AN AFRICAN #METOO MOVEMENT

TOUFAH

Toufah
Jallow
with Kim Pittaway

T2P BOOKS // TRUTHFUL NARRATIVES = BETTER UNDERSTANDING

"Hope finds a prominent presence in what so many think is a hopeless, endless conflict."
— *KIRKUS*

FRIENDLY FIRE
A MEMOIR

How Israel Became Its Own Worst
Enemy and the Hope for Its Future

AMI AYALON

WITH
ANTHONY DAVID

INTRODUCTION BY
DENNIS ROSS

T2P BOOKS // TRUTHFUL NARRATIVES = BETTER UNDERSTANDING

"A book that is both a history and a sports classic." — *DETROIT FREE PRESS*
"One of the most compelling sports biographies [ever]. A must-read."
— (starred review) *BOOKLIST*

HARD DRIVING
THE WENDELL SCOTT STORY

The American Odyssey of
NASCAR's First Black Driver

BRIAN DONOVAN

FOREWORD BY
JOE POSNANSKI

T2P BOOKS // TRUTHFUL NARRATIVES = BETTER UNDERSTANDING

"[A] nuanced, open-minded, de-politicized discussion of our post-#MeToo world."
— *REFINERY29*

HAD IT COMING

Rape Culture Meets #MeToo:
Now What?

ROBYN DOOLITTLE

Steerforth Press
Truth to Power Books

TRUTH
TO
POWER

"A must read for nonhistorians seeking a firm grasp of accurate American history."
— *KIRKUS REVIEWS*

A TRUE HISTORY
OF THE UNITED STATES

Indigenous Genocide, Racialized Slavery, Hyper-Capitalism, Militarist Imperialism, and Other Overlooked Aspects of American Exceptionalism

DANIEL A. SJURSEN

T2P BOOKS // TRUTHFUL NARRATIVES = BETTER UNDERSTANDING

"This moving and sprightly book is filled with backstories from America's struggle for religious freedom that I'll bet you have never heard before . . . a brilliant scholar's telling insights on the right way for church, state, and society to interact."
— E.J. DIONNE JR., AUTHOR OF *CODE RED* AND *WHY THE RIGHT WENT WRONG*

SOLEMN REVERENCE

THE SEPARATION OF CHURCH AND STATE IN AMERICAN LIFE

RANDALL BALMER

T2P BOOKS // TRUTHFUL NARRATIVES = BETTER UNDERSTANDING

"Margaret Kimberley gives us an intellectual gem of prophetic fire about all the US presidents and their deep roots in the vicious legacy of white supremacy and predatory capitalism. Such truths seem more than most Americans can bear, though we ignore her words at our own peril!"
—CORNEL WEST, AUTHOR OF *RACE MATTERS*

PREJUDENTIAL

BLACK AMERICA AND THE PRESIDENTS

MARGARET KIMBERLEY

T2P BOOKS // TRUTHFUL NARRATIVES = BETTER UNDERSTANDING

"Investigative journalism at its relentless and compassionate best." — *KIRKUS REVIEWS*
"Methamphetamine was a huge part of this case . . . A horrible murder driven by drugs."
— PROSECUTOR CAL RERUCHA
"A gripping read." — *PEOPLE MAGAZINE*

THE BOOK OF MATT

THE REAL STORY OF THE MURDER OF MATTHEW SHEPARD

STEPHEN JIMENEZ

NEW INTRODUCTION BY
ANDREW SULLIVAN

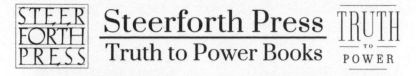

"This short, powerful book should be required reading for anyone who has ever wondered what it's like to be an ordinary citizen living in a war zone." — *PUBLISHERS WEEKLY*

WHEN THE BULBUL STOPPED SINGING

LIFE IN PALESTINE DURING AN ISRAELI SIEGE

RAJA SHEHADEH

NEW INTRODUCTION BY
COLUM McCANN

One of three books people "should read to understand what happened in Vietnam."
—*THE MARINE CORPS GAZETTE*

WAR OF NUMBERS

AN INTELLIGENCE MEMOIR OF THE VIETNAM WAR'S UNCOUNTED ENEMY

SAM ADAMS

FOREWORD BY
COL. DAVID HACKWORTH

NEW INTRODUCTION BY
JOHN PRADOS